Frederick Winslow Taylor

The Principles of Scientific Management

first published in 1911

1ST.PAGE CLASSICS

Visit us on *Facebook* and *YouTube*:

Ocean of Minds Media House

The Principles of Scientific Management
was originally published in 1911

Author:
Frederick Winslow Taylor

Cover Image:

Published 2020 by *1st. Page Classics*,
a Series of *Ocean of Minds Media House*

Publisher:
Ocean of Minds Media House Ltd.
R.R. #2, River Denys
Nova Scotia B0E 2Y0, Canada

www.oceanofmindsmedia.com
oceanofmindsmedia@gmail.com

Printed and Distributed by:
amazon.com Inc.
410 Terry Avenue, North
Seattle, WA 98109-5210, USA

ISBN: 978-1-7771829-1-5

In Memoriam

Frederick Winslow Taylor

March 20, 1856 in Germantown, Pennsylvania –
March 21, 1915 in Philadelphia

Frederick Winslow Taylor was one of the intellectual leaders of the so-called *efficiency movement* and his ideas were highly influential in the progressive era beginning in the 1890s. Taylor summed up his efficiency techniques in *The Principles of Scientific Management* in 1911. Frederick Winslow Taylor was also an mechanical engineer who sought to improve industrial efficiency.

Introduction

President Roosevelt, in his address to the Governors at the White House, prophetically remarked that "The conservation of our national resources is only preliminary to the larger question of national efficiency." The whole country at once recognized the importance of conserving our material resources and a large movement has been started which will be effective in accomplishing this object. As yet, however, we have but vaguely appreciated the importance of "the larger question of increasing our national efficiency."

We can see our forests vanishing, our water-powers going to waste, our soil being carried by floods into the sea; and the end of our coal and our iron is in sight. But our larger wastes of human effort, which go on every day through such of our acts as are blundering, ill-directed, or inefficient, and which Mr. Roosevelt refers to as a lack of "national efficiency," are less visible, less tangible, and are but vaguely appreciated.

We can see and feel the waste of material things. Awkward, inefficient, or ill-directed movements of men, however, leave nothing visible or tangible behind them. Their appreciation calls for an act of memory, an effort of the imagination. And for this reason, even though our daily loss from this source is greater than from our waste of material things, the one has stirred us deeply, while the other has moved us but little.

As yet there has been no public agitation for "greater national efficiency," no meetings have been called to consider how this is to be brought about. And still there are signs that the need for greater efficiency is widely felt.

The search for better, for more competent men, from the presidents of our great companies down to our household servants, was never more vigorous than it is now. And more than ever before is the demand for competent men in excess of the supply.

What we are all looking for, however, is the ready-made, competent man; the man whom some one else has trained. It is only when we fully realize that our duty, as well as our opportunity, lies in systematically cooperating to train and to make this competent man, instead of in hunting for a man whom some one else has trained, that we shall be on the road to national efficiency.

In the past the prevailing idea has been well expressed in the saying that "Captains of industry are born, not made"; and the theory has been that if one could get the right man, methods could be safely left to him. In the future it will be appreciated that our leaders must be trained right as well as born right, and that no great man can (with the old system of personal management) hope to compete with a number of ordinary men who have been properly organized so as efficiently to cooperate.

In the past the man has been first; in the future the system must be first. This in no sense, however, implies that great men are not needed. On the contrary, the first object of any good system must be that of developing first-class men; and under systematic management the best man rises to the top more certainly and more rapidly than ever before.

This paper has been written:

First. To point out, through a series of simple illustrations, the great loss which the whole country is suffering through inefficiency in almost all of our daily acts.

Second. To try to convince the reader that the remedy for this inefficiency lies in systematic management, rather than in searching for some unusual or extraordinary man.

Third. To prove that the best management is a true science, resting upon clearly defined laws, rules, and principles, as a foundation. And further to show that the fundamental principles of scientific management are applicable to all kinds of human activities, from our simplest individual acts to the work of our great corporations, which call for the most elaborate cooperation. And, briefly, through a series of illustrations, to convince the reader that whenever these principles are correctly applied, results must follow which are truly astounding.

This paper was originally prepared for presentation to *The American Society of Mechanical Engineers*. The illustrations chosen are such as, it is believed, will especially appeal to engineers and to managers of industrial and manufacturing establishments, and also quite as much to all of the men who are working in these establishments. It is hoped, however, that it will be clear to other readers that the same principles can be applied with equal force to all social activities: to the management of our homes; the management of our farms; the management of the business of our tradesmen, large and small; of our churches, our philanthropic institutions, our universities, and our governmental departments.

Chapter I

Fundamentals of Scientific Management

The principal object of management should be to secure the maximum prosperity for the employer, coupled with the maximum prosperity for each employé. The words "maximum prosperity" are used, in their broad sense, to mean not only large dividends for the company or owner, but the development of every branch of the business to its highest state of excellence, so that the prosperity may be permanent.

In the same way maximum prosperity for each employé means not only higher wages than are usually received by men of his class, but, of more importance still, it also means the development of each man to his state of maximum efficiency, so that he may be able to do, generally speaking, the highest grade of work for which his natural abilities fit him, and it further means giving him, when possible, this class of work to do.

It would seem to be so self-evident that maximum prosperity for the employer, coupled with maximum prosperity for the employé, ought to be the two leading objects of management, that even to state this fact should be unnecessary. And yet there is no question that, throughout the industrial world, a large part of the organization of employers, as well as employés, is for war rather than for peace, and that perhaps the majority on either side do not believe that it is possible so to arrange their mutual relations that their interests become identical.

The majority of these men believe that the fundamental interests of employés and employers are necessarily antagonistic. Scientific management, on the contrary, has for its very foundation the firm conviction that the true interests of the two are one and the same; that prosperity for the employer cannot exist through a long term of years unless it is accompanied by prosperity for the employé, and *vice versa*; and that it is possible to give the workman what he most wants – high wages – and the employer what he wants – a low labor cost – for his manufactures.

It is hoped that some at least of those who do not sympathize with each of these objects may be led to modify their views; that some employers, whose attitude toward their workmen has been that of trying to get the largest amount of work out of them for the smallest possible wages, may be led to see that a more liberal policy toward their men will pay them better; and that some of those workmen who begrudge a fair and even a large profit to their employers, and who feel that all of the fruits of their labor should belong to them, and that those for whom they work and the capital invested in the business are entitled to little or nothing, may be led to modify these views.

No one can be found who will deny that in the case of any single individual the greatest prosperity can exist only when that individual has reached his highest state of efficiency; that is, when he is turning out his largest daily output.

The truth of this fact is also perfectly clear in the case of two men working together. To illustrate: if you and your workman have become so skilful that you and he together are making two pairs of shoes in a day, while your competitor and his workman are making only one pair, it is clear that after selling your two pairs of shoes you can pay your workman much higher wages than your competitor who produces only one pair of shoes is able to pay his man, and that there will still be enough money left over for you to have a larger profit than your competitor.

In the case of a more complicated manufacturing establishment, it should also be perfectly clear that the greatest permanent prosperity for the workman, coupled with the greatest prosperity for the employer, can be brought about only when the work of the establishment is done with the smallest combined expenditure of human effort, plus nature's resources, plus the cost for the use of capital in the shape of machines, buildings, etc. Or, to state the same thing in a different way: that the greatest prosperity can exist only as the result of the greatest possible productivity of the men and machines of the establishment – that is, when each man and each machine are turning out the largest possible output; because unless your men and your machines are daily turning out more work than others around you, it is clear that competition will prevent your paying higher wages to your workmen than are paid to those of your competitor. And what is true as to the possibility of paying high wages in the case of two companies competing close beside one another is also true as to whole districts of the country and even as to nations which are in competition. In a word, that maximum prosperity can exist only as the result of maximum productivity. Later in this paper illustrations will be given of several companies which are earning large dividends and at the same time paying from 30 per cent. to 100 per cent. higher wages to their men than are paid to similar men immediately around them, and with whose employers they are in competition. These illustrations will cover different types of work, from the most elementary to the most complicated.

If the above reasoning is correct, it follows that the most important object of both the workmen and the management should be the training and development of each individual in the establishment, so that he can do (at his fastest pace and with the maximum of efficiency) the highest class of work for which his natural abilities fit him.

These principles appear to be so self-evident that many men may think it almost childish to state them. Let us, however, turn to the facts, as they actually exist in this country and in England. The English and American peoples are the greatest sportsmen in the world. Whenever an American workman plays baseball, or an English workman plays cricket, it is safe to say that he strains every nerve to secure victory for his side. He does his very best to make the largest possible number of runs. The universal sentiment is so strong that any man who fails to give out all there is in him in sport is branded as a "quitter," and treated with contempt by those who are around him.

When the same workman returns to work on the following day, instead of using every effort to turn out the largest possible amount of work, in a majority of the cases this man deliberately plans to do as little as he safely can – to turn out far less work than he is well able to do – in many instances to do not more than one-third to one-half of a proper day's work. And in fact if he were to do his best to turn out his largest possible day's work, he would be abused by his fellow-workers for so doing, even more than if he had proved himself a "quitter" in sport. Underworking, that is, deliberately working slowly so as to avoid doing a full day's work, "soldiering," as it is called in this country, "hanging it out," as it is called in England, "ca canae," as it is called in Scotland, is almost universal in industrial establishments, and prevails also to a large extent in the building trades; and the writer asserts without fear of contradiction that this constitutes the greatest evil with which the working-people of both England and America are now afflicted.

It will be shown later in this paper that doing away with slow working and "soldiering" in all its forms and so arranging the relations between employer and employé that each workman will work to his very best advantage and at his best speed, accompanied by the intimate cooperation with the management and the help (which the workman should receive) from the management, would result on the average in nearly doubling the output of each man and each machine. What other reforms, among those which are being discussed by these two nations, could do as much toward promoting prosperity, toward the diminution of poverty, and the alleviation of suffering? America and England have been recently agitated over such subjects as the tariff, the control of the large corporations on the one hand, and of hereditary power on the other hand, and over various more or less socialistic proposals for taxation, etc. On these subjects both peoples have been profoundly stirred, and yet hardly a voice has been raised to call attention to this vastly greater and more important subject of "soldiering," which directly and powerfully affects the wages, the prosperity, and the life of almost every working-man, and also quite as much the prosperity of every industrial establishment in the nation.

The elimination of "soldiering" and of the several causes of slow working would so lower the cost of production that both our home and foreign markets would be greatly enlarged, and we could compete on more than even terms with our rivals. It would remove one of the fundamental causes for dull times, for lack of employment, and for poverty, and therefore would have a more permanent and far-reaching effect upon these misfortunes than any of the curative remedies that are now being used to soften their consequences. It would insure higher wages and make shorter working hours and better working and home conditions possible.

Why is it, then, in the face of the self-evident fact that maximum prosperity can exist only as the result of the determined effort of each workman to turn out each day his largest possible day's work, that the great majority of our men are deliberately doing just the opposite, and that even when the men have the best of intentions their work is in most cases far from efficient? There are three causes for this condition, which may be briefly summarized as:

First. The fallacy, which has from time immemorial been almost universal among workmen, that a material increase in the output of each man or each machine in the trade would result in the end in throwing a large number of men out of work.

Second. The defective systems of management which are in common use, and which make it necessary for each workman to soldier, or work slowly, in order that he may protect his own best interests.

Third. The inefficient rule-of-thumb methods, which are still almost universal in all trades, and in practising which our workmen waste a large part of their effort.

This paper will attempt to show the enormous gains which would result from the substitution by our workmen of scientific for rule-of-thumb methods. To explain a little more fully these three causes:

First. The great majority of workmen still believe that if they were to work at their best speed they would be doing a great injustice to the whole trade by throwing a lot of men out of work, and yet the history of the development of each trade shows that each improvement, whether it be the invention of a new machine or the introduction of a better method, which results in increasing the productive capacity of the men in the trade and cheapening the costs, instead of throwing men out of work make in the end work for more men.

The cheapening of any article in common use almost immediately results in a largely increased demand for that article. Take the case of shoes, for instance. The introduction of machinery for doing every element of the work which was formerly done by hand has resulted in making shoes at a fraction of their former labor cost, and in selling them so cheap that now almost every man, woman, and child in the working-classes buys one or two pairs of shoes per year, and wears shoes all the time, whereas formerly each workman bought perhaps one pair of shoes every five years, and went barefoot most of the time, wearing shoes only as a luxury or as a matter of the sternest necessity. In spite of the enormously increased output of shoes per workman, which has come with shoe machinery, the demand for shoes has so increased that there are relatively more men working in the shoe industry now than ever before.

The workmen in almost every trade have before them an object lesson of this kind, and yet, because they are ignorant of the history of their own trade even, they still firmly believe, as their fathers did before them, that it is against their best interests for each man to turn out each day as much work as possible.

Under this fallacious idea a large proportion of the workmen of both countries each day deliberately work slowly so as to curtail the output. Almost every labor union has made, or is contemplating making, rules which have for their object curtailing the output of their members, and those men who have the greatest influence with the working-people, the labor leaders as well as many people with philanthropic feelings who are helping them, are daily spreading this fallacy and at the same time telling them that they are overworked.

A great deal has been and is being constantly said about "sweatshop" work and conditions. The writer has great sympathy with those who are overworked, but on the whole a greater sympathy for those who are *under paid*. For every individual, however, who is overworked, there are a hundred who intentionally underwork – greatly underwork – every day of their lives, and who for this reason deliberately aid in establishing those conditions which in the end inevitably result in low wages. And yet hardly a single voice is being raised in an endeavor to correct this evil.

As engineers and managers, we are more intimately acquainted with these facts than any other class in the community, and are therefore best fitted to lead in a movement to combat this fallacious idea by educating not only the workmen but the whole of the country as to the true facts. And yet we are practically doing nothing in this direction, and are leaving this field entirely in the hands of the labor agitators (many of whom are misinformed and misguided), and of sentimentalists who are ignorant as to actual working conditions.

Second. As to the second cause for soldiering – the relations which exist between employers and employés under almost all of the systems of management which are in common use – it is impossible in a few words to make it clear to one not familiar with this problem why it is that the *ignorance of employers* as to the proper time in which work of various kinds should be done makes it for the interest of the workman to "soldier."

The writer therefore quotes herewith from a paper read before The American Society of Mechanical Engineers, in June, 1903, entitled "Shop Management," which it is hoped will explain fully this cause for soldiering:

"This loafing or soldiering proceeds from two causes. First, from the natural instinct and tendency of men to take it easy, which may be called natural soldiering. Second, from more intricate second thought and reasoning caused by their relations with other men, which may be called systematic soldiering.

"There is no question that the tendency of the average man (in all walks of life) is toward working at a slow, easy gait, and that it is only after a good deal of thought and observation on his part or as a result of example, conscience, or external pressure that he takes a more rapid pace. "There are, of course, men of unusual energy, vitality, and ambition who naturally choose the fastest gait, who set up their own standards, and who work hard, even though it may be against their best interests. But these few uncommon men only serve by forming a contrast to emphasize the tendency of the average.

"This common tendency to 'take it easy' is greatly increased by bringing a number of men together on similar work and at a uniform standard rate of pay by the day.

"Under this plan the better men gradually but surely slow down their gait to that of the poorest and least efficient. When a naturally energetic man works for a few days beside a lazy one, the logic of the situation is unanswerable. 'Why should I work hard when that lazy fellow gets the same pay that I do and does only half as much work?'

"A careful time study of men working under these conditions will disclose facts which are ludicrous as well as pitiable.

"To illustrate: The writer has timed a naturally energetic workman who, while going and coming from work, would walk at a speed of from three to four miles per hour, and not infrequently trot home after a day's work. On arriving at his work he would immediately slow down to a speed of about one mile an hour. When, for example, wheeling a loaded wheelbarrow, he would go at a good fast pace even up hill in order to be as short a time as possible under load, and immediately on the return walk slow down to a mile an hour, improving every opportunity for delay short of actually sitting down. In order to be sure not to do more than his lazy neighbor, he would actually tire himself in his effort to go slow.

"These men were working under a foreman of good reputation and highly thought of by his employer, who, when his attention was called to this state of things, answered: 'Well, I can keep them from sitting down, but the devil can't make them get a move on while they are at work.'

"The natural laziness of men is serious, but by far the greatest evil from which both workmen and employers are suffering is the *systematic soldiering* which is almost universal under all of the ordinary schemes of management and which results from a careful study on the part of the workmen of what will promote their best interests.

"The writer was much interested recently in hearing one small but experienced golf caddy boy of twelve explaining to a green caddy, who had shown special energy and interest, the necessity of going slow and lagging behind his man when he came up to the ball, showing him that since they were paid by the hour, the faster they went the less money they got, and finally telling him that if he went too fast the other boys would give him a licking.

"This represents a type of *systematic soldiering* which is not, however, very serious, since it is done with the knowledge of the employer, who can quite easily break it up if he wishes.

"The greater part of the *systematic soldiering*, however, is done by the men with the deliberate object of keeping their employers ignorant of how fast work can be done.

"So universal is soldiering for this purpose that hardly a competent workman can be found in a large establishment, whether he works by the day or on piece work, contract work, or under any of the ordinary systems, who does not devote a considerable part of his time to studying just how slow he can work and still convince his employer that he is going at a good pace.

"The causes for this are, briefly, that practically all employers determine upon a maximum sum which they feel it is right for each of their classes of employees to earn per day, whether their men work by the day or piece.

"Each workman soon finds out about what this figure is for his particular case, and he also realizes that when his employer is convinced that a man is capable of doing more work than he has done, he will find sooner or later some way of compelling him to do it with little or no increase of pay.

"Employers derive their knowledge of how much of a given class of work can be done in a day from either their own experience, which has frequently grown hazy with age, from casual and unsystematic observation of their men, or at best from records which are kept, showing the quickest time in which each job has been done. In many cases the employer will feel almost certain that a given job can be done faster than it has been, but he rarely cares to take the drastic measures necessary to force men to do it in the quickest time, unless he has an actual record proving conclusively how fast the work can be done.

"It evidently becomes for each man's interest, then, to see that no job is done faster than it has been in the past. The younger and less experienced men are taught this by their elders, and all possible persuasion and social pressure is brought to bear upon the greedy and selfish men to keep them from making new records which result in temporarily increasing their wages, while all those who come after them are made to work harder for the same old pay.

"Under the best day work of the ordinary type, when accurate records are kept of the amount of work done by each man and of his efficiency, and when each man's wages are raised as he improves, and those who fail to rise to a certain standard are discharged and a fresh supply of carefully selected men are given work in their places, both the natural loafing and systematic soldiering can be largely broken up. This can only be done, however, when the men are thoroughly convinced that there is no intention of establishing piece work even in the remote future, and it is next to impossible to make men believe this when the work is of such a nature that they believe piece work to be practicable. In most cases their fear of making a record which will be used as a basis for piece work will cause them to soldier as much as they dare.

"It is, however, under piece work that the art of systematic soldiering is thoroughly developed; after a workman has had the price per piece of the work he is doing lowered two or three times as a result of his having worked harder and increased his output, he is likely entirely to lose sight of his employer's side of the case and become imbued with a grim determination to have no more cuts if soldiering can prevent it. Unfortunately for the character of the workman, soldiering involves a deliberate attempt to mislead and deceive his employer, and thus upright and straightforward workmen are compelled to become more or less hypocritical. The employer is soon looked upon as an antagonist, if not an enemy, and the mutual confidence which should exist between a leader and his men, the enthusiasm, the feeling that they are all working for the same end and will share in the results is entirely lacking.

"The feeling of antagonism under the ordinary piece-work system becomes in many cases so marked on the part of the men that any proposition made by their employers, however reasonable, is looked upon with suspicion, and soldiering becomes such a fixed habit that men will frequently take pains to restrict the product of machines which they are running when even a large increase in output would involve no more work on their part."

Third. As to the third cause for slow work, considerable space will later in this paper be devoted to illustrating the great gain, both to employers and employés, which results from the substitution of scientific for rule-of-thumb methods in even the smallest details of the work of every trade. The enormous saving of time and therefore increase in the output which it is possible to effect through eliminating unnecessary motions and substituting fast for slow and inefficient motions for the men working in any of our trades can be fully realized only after one has personally seen the improvement which results from a thorough motion and time study, made by a competent man.

To explain briefly: owing to the fact that the workmen in all of our trades have been taught the details of their work by observation of those immediately around them, there are many different ways in common use for doing the same thing, perhaps forty, fifty, or a hundred ways of doing each act in each trade, and for the same reason there is a great variety in the implements used for each class of work. Now, among the various methods and implements used in each element of each trade there is always one method and one implement which is quicker and better than any of the rest. And this one best method and best implement can only be discovered or developed through a scientific study and analysis of all of the methods and implements in use, together with accurate, minute, motion and time study. This involves the gradual substitution of science for rule of thumb throughout the mechanic arts.

This paper will show that the underlying philosophy of all of the old systems of management in common use makes it imperative that each workman shall be left with the final responsibility for doing his job practically as he thinks best, with comparatively little help and advice from the management. And it will also show that because of this isolation of workmen, it is in most cases impossible for the men working under these systems to do their work in accordance with the rules and laws of a science or art, even where one exists.

The writer asserts as a general principle (and he proposes to give illustrations tending to prove the fact later in this paper) that in almost all of the mechanic arts the science which underlies each act of each workman is so great and amounts to so much that the workman who is best suited to actually doing the work is incapable of fully understanding this science, without the guidance and help of those who are working with him or over him, either through lack of education or through insufficient mental capacity. In order that the work may be done in accordance with scientific laws, it is necessary that there shall be a far more equal division of the responsibility between the management and the workmen than exists under any of the ordinary types of management. Those in the management whose duty it is to develop this science should also guide and help the workman in working under it, and should assume a much larger share of the responsibility for results than under usual conditions is assumed by the management. The body of this paper will make it clear that, to work according to scientific laws, the management must take over and perform much of the work which is now left to the men; almost every act of the workman should be preceded by one or more preparatory acts of the management which enable him to do his work better and quicker than he otherwise could. And each man should daily be taught by and receive the most friendly help from those who are over him, instead of being, at the one extreme, driven or coerced by his bosses, and at the other left to his own unaided devices.

This close, intimate, personal cooperation between the management and the men is of the essence of modern scientific or task management. It will be shown by a series of practical illustrations that, through this friendly cooperation, namely, through sharing equally in every day's burden, all of the great obstacles (above described) to obtaining the maximum, output for each man and each machine in the establishment are swept away. The 30 per cent. to 100 per cent. increase in wages which the workmen are able to earn beyond what they receive under the old type of management, coupled with the daily intimate shoulder to shoulder contact with the management, entirely removes all cause for soldiering. And in a few years, under this system, the workmen have before them the object lesson of seeing that a great increase in the output per man results in giving employment to more men, instead of throwing men out of work, thus completely eradicating the fallacy that a larger output for each man will throw other men out of work.

It is the writer's judgment, then, that while much can be done and should be done by writing and talking toward educating not only workmen, but all classes in the community, as to the importance of obtaining the maximum output of each man and each machine, it is only through the adoption of modern scientific management that this great problem can be finally solved. Probably most of the readers of this paper will say that all of this is mere theory. On the contrary, the theory, or philosophy, of scientific management is just beginning to be understood, whereas the management itself has been a gradual evolution, extending over a period of nearly thirty years. And during this time the employés of one company after another, including a large range and diversity of industries, have gradually changed from the ordinary to the scientific type of management. At least 50,000 workmen in the United States are now employed under this system; and they are receiving from 30 per cent. to 100 per cent. higher wages daily than are paid to men of similar caliber with whom they are surrounded, while the companies employing them are more prosperous than ever before. In these companies the output, per man and per machine, has on an average been doubled. During all these years there has never been a single strike among the men working under this system. In place of the suspicious watchfulness and the more or less open warfare which characterizes the ordinary types of management, there is universally friendly cooperation between the management and the men.

Several papers have been written, describing the expedients which have been adopted and the details which have been developed under scientific management and the steps to be taken in changing from the ordinary to the scientific type. But unfortunately most of the readers of these papers have mistaken the

mechanism for the true essence. Scientific management fundamentally consists of certain broad general principles, a certain philosophy, which can be applied in many ways, and a description of what any one man or men may believe to be the best mechanism for applying these general principles should in no way be confused with the principles themselves.

It is not here claimed that any single panacea exists for all of the troubles of the working-people or of employers. As long as some people are born lazy or inefficient, and others are born greedy and brutal, as long as vice and crime are with us, just so long will a certain amount of poverty, misery, and unhappiness be with us also. No system of management, no single expedient within the control of any man or any set of men can insure continuous prosperity to either workmen or employers. Prosperity depends upon so many factors entirely beyond the control of any one set of men, any state, or even any one country, that certain periods will inevitably come when both sides must suffer, more or less. It is claimed, however, that under scientific management the intermediate periods will be far more prosperous, far happier, and more free from discord and dissension. And also, that the periods will be fewer, shorter and the suffering less. And this will be particularly true in any one town, any one section of the country, or any one state which first substitutes the principles of scientific management for the rule of thumb.

That these principles are certain to come into general use practically throughout the civilized world, sooner or later, the writer is profoundly convinced, and the sooner they come the better for all the people.

Chapter II

THE PRINCIPLES OF SCIENTIFIC MANAGEMENT

The writer has found that there are three questions uppermost in the minds of men when they become interested in scientific management.

First. Wherein do the principles of scientific management differ essentially from those of ordinary management?

Second. Why are better results attained under scientific management than under the other types?

Third. Is not the most important problem that of getting the right man at the head of the company? And If you have the right man cannot the choice of the type of management be safely left to him?

One of the principal objects of the following pages will be to give a satisfactory answer to these questions.

THE FINEST TYPE OF ORDINARY MANAGEMENT

Before starting to illustrate the principles of scientific management, or "task management" as it is briefly called, it seems desirable to outline what the writer believes will be recognized as the best type of management which is in common use. This is done so that the great difference between the best of the ordinary management and scientific management may be fully appreciated. In an industrial establishment which employs say from 500 to 1000

workmen, there will be found in many cases at least twenty to thirty different trades. The workmen in each of these trades have had their knowledge handed down to them by word of mouth, through the many years in which their trade has been developed from the primitive condition, in which our far-distant ancestors each one practised the rudiments of many different trades, to the present state of great and growing subdivision of labor, in which each man specializes upon some comparatively small class of work.

The ingenuity of each generation has developed quicker and better methods for doing every element of the work in every trade. Thus the methods which are now in use may in a broad sense be said to be an evolution representing the survival of the fittest and best of the ideas which have been developed since the starting of each trade. However, while this is true in a broad sense, only those who are intimately acquainted with each of these trades are fully aware of the fact that in hardly any element of any trade is there uniformity in the methods which are used. Instead of having only one way which is generally accepted as a standard, there are in daily use, say, fifty or a hundred different ways of doing each element of the work. And a little thought will make it clear that this must inevitably be the case, since our methods have been handed down from man to man by word of mouth, or have, in most cases, been almost unconsciously learned through personal observation. Practically in no instances have they been codified or systematically analyzed or described. The ingenuity and experience of each generation – of each decade, even, have without doubt handed over better methods to the next. This mass of rule-of -thumb or traditional knowledge may be said to be the principal asset or possession of every tradesman. Now, in the best of the ordinary types of management, the managers recognize frankly the fact that the 500 or 1000 workmen, included in the twenty to thirty trades, who are under them, possess this mass of traditional knowledge, a large part of which is not in the possession of the management. The management, of course, includes foremen and superintendents, who themselves have been in most cases first-class workers at their trades. And yet these foremen and superintendents know, better than any one else, that their own knowledge and personal skill falls far short of the combined knowledge and dexterity of all the workmen under them. The most experienced managers therefore frankly place before their workmen the problem of doing the work in the best and most economical way. They recognize the task before them as that of inducing each workman to use his best endeavors, his hardest work, all his traditional knowledge, his skill, his ingenuity, and his good-will – in a word, his "initiative," so as to yield the largest possible return to his employer. The problem before the management, then, may be briefly said to be that of obtaining the best *initiative* of every workman. And the writer uses the word "initiative" in its broadest sense, to cover all of the good qualities sought for from the men.

On the other hand, no intelligent manager would hope to obtain in any full measure the initiative of his workmen unless he felt that he was giving them something more than they usually receive from their employers. Only those among the readers of this paper who have been managers or who have worked themselves at a trade realize how far the average workman falls short of giving his employer his full initiative. It is well within the mark to state that in nineteen out of twenty industrial establishments the workmen believe it to be directly against their interests to give their employers their best initiative, and that instead of working hard to do the largest possible amount of work and the best quality of work for their employers, they deliberately work as slowly as they dare while they at the same time try to make those over them believe that they are working fast.

The writer repeats, therefore, that in order to have any hope of obtaining the initiative of his workmen the manager must give some *special incentive* to his men beyond that which is given to the average of the trade. This incentive can be given in several different ways, as, for example, the hope of rapid promotion or advancement; higher wages, either in the form of generous piece-work prices or of a premium or bonus of some kind for good and rapid work; shorter hours of labor; better surroundings and working conditions than are ordinarily given, etc., and, above all, this special incentive should be accompanied by that personal consideration for, and friendly contact with, his workmen which comes only from a genuine and kindly interest in the welfare of those under him. It is only by giving a special inducement or "incentive" of this kind that the employer can hope even approximately to get the "initiative" of his workmen. Under the ordinary type of management the necessity for offering the workman a special inducement has come to be so generally recognized that a large proportion of those most interested in the subject look upon the adoption of some one of the modern schemes for paying men (such as piece work, the premium plan, or the bonus plan, for instance) as practically the whole system of management. Under scientific management, however, the particular pay system which is adopted is merely one of the subordinate elements.

Broadly speaking, then; the best type of management in ordinary use may be defined as management in which the workmen give their best *initiative* and in return receive some *special incentive* from their employers. This type of management will be referred to as the management of *initiative and incentive* in contradistinction to scientific management, or task management, with which it is to be compared.

The writer hopes that the management of "initiative and incentive" will be recognized as representing the best type in ordinary use, and in fact he believes that it will be hard to persuade the average manager that anything better exists in the whole field than this type. The task which the writer has before him, then, is the difficult one of trying to prove in a thoroughly convincing way that there is another type of management which is not only better but overwhelmingly better than the management of "initiative and incentive."

The universal prejudice in favor of the management of "initiative and incentive" is so strong that no mere theoretical advantages which can be pointed out will be likely to convince the average manager that any other system is better. It will be upon a series of practical illustrations of the actual working of the two systems that the writer will depend in his efforts to prove that scientific management is so greatly superior to other types. Certain elementary principles, a certain philosophy, will however be recognized as the essence of that which is being illustrated in all of the practical examples which will be given. And the broad principles in which the scientific system differs from the ordinary or "rule-of-thumb" system are so simple in their nature that it seems desirable to describe them before starting with the illustrations.

Under the old type of management success depends almost entirely upon getting the "initiative" of the workmen, and it is indeed a rare case in which this initiative is really attained. Under scientific management the "initiative" of the workmen (that is, their hard work, their good-will, and their ingenuity) is obtained with absolute uniformity and to a greater extent than is possible under the old system; and in addition to this improvement on the part of the men, the managers assume new burdens, new duties, and responsibilities never dreamed of in the past. The managers assume, for instance, the burden of gathering together all of the traditional knowledge which in the past has been possessed by the workmen and then of classifying, tabulating, and reducing this knowledge to rules, laws, and formulæ which are immensely helpful to the workmen in doing their daily work. In addition to developing a science in this way, the management take on three other types of duties which involve new and heavy burdens for themselves. These new duties are grouped under four heads:

First. They develop a science for each element of a man's work, which replaces the old rule-of-thumb method.

Second. They scientifically select and then train, teach, and develop the workman, whereas in the past he chose his own work and trained himself as best he could.

Third. They heartily cooperate with the men so as to insure all of the work being done in accordance with the principles of the science which has been developed.

Fourth. There is an almost equal division of the work and the responsibility between the management and the workmen. The management take over all work for which they are better fitted than the workmen, while in the past almost all of the work and the greater part of the responsibility were thrown upon the men.

It is this combination of the initiative of the workmen, coupled with the new types of work done by the management, that makes scientific management so much more efficient than the old plan. Three of these elements exist in many cases, under the management of "initiative and incentive," in a small and rudimentary way, but they are, under this management, of minor importance, whereas under scientific management they form the very essence of the whole system.

The fourth of these elements, "an almost equal division of the responsibility between the management and the workmen," requires further explanation. The philosophy of the management of "initiative and incentive" makes it necessary for each workman to bear almost the entire responsibility for the general plan as well as for each detail of his work, and in many cases for his implements as well. In addition to this he must do all of the actual physical labor. The development of a science, on the other hand, involves the establishment of many rules, laws, and formulæ which replace the judgment of the individual workman and which can be effectively used only after having been systematically recorded, indexed, etc. The practical use of scientific data also calls for a room in which to keep the books, records, etc., and a desk for the planner to work at. Thus all of the planning which under the old system was done by the workman, as a result of his personal experience, must of necessity under the new system be done by the management in accordance with the laws of the science; because even if the workman was well suited to the development and use of scientific data, it would be physically impossible for him to work at his machine and at a desk at the same time. It is also clear that in most cases one type of man is needed to plan ahead and an entirely different type to execute the work.

The man in the planning room, whose specialty under scientific management is planning ahead, invariably finds that the work can be done better and more economically by a subdivision of the labor; each act of each mechanic, for example, should be preceded by various preparatory acts done by other men. And all of this involves, as we have said, "an almost equal division of the responsibihty and the work between the management and the workman."

To summarize: Under the management of "initiative and incentive" practically the whole problem is "up to the workman," while under scientific management fully one-half of the problem is "up to the management."

Perhaps the most prominent single element in modern scientific management is the task idea. The work of every workman is fully planned out by the management at least one day in advance, and each man receives in most cases complete written instructions, describing in detail the task which he is to accomplish, as well as the means to be used in doing the work. And the work planned in advance in this way constitutes a task which is to be solved, as explained above, not by the workman alone, but in almost all cases by the joint effort of the workman and the management. This task specifies not only what is to be done but how it is to be done and the exact time allowed for doing it. And whenever the workman succeeds in doing his task right, and within the time limit specified, he receives an addition of from 30 per cent. to 100 per cent. to his ordinary wages. These tasks are carefully planned, so that both good and careful work are called for in their performance, but it should be distinctly understood that in no case is the workman called upon to work at a pace which would be injurious to his health. The task is always so regulated that the man who is well suited to his job will thrive while working at this rate during a long term of years and grow happier and more prosperous, instead of being overworked. Scientific management consists very largely in preparing for and carrying out these tasks.

The writer is fully aware that to perhaps most of the readers of this paper the four elements which differentiate the new management from the old will at first appear to be merely high-sounding phrases; and he would again repeat that he has no idea of convincing the reader of their value merely through announcing their existence. His hope of carrying conviction rests upon demonstrating the tremendous force and effect of these four elements through a series of practical illustrations. It will be shown, first, that they can be applied absolutely to all classes of work, from the most elementary to the most intricate; and second, that when they are applied, the results must of necessity be overwhelmingly greater than those which it is possible to attain under the management of initiative and incentive. The first illustration is that of handling pig iron, and this work is chosen because it is typical of perhaps the crudest and most elementary form of labor which is performed by man. This work is done by men with no other implements than their hands. The pig-iron handler stoops down, picks up a pig weighing about 92 pounds, walks for a few feet or yards and then drops it on to the ground or upon a pile. This work is so crude and elementary in its nature that the writer firmly believes that it would be possible to train an intelligent gorilla so as to become a more efficient pig-iron handler than any man can be. Yet it will be shown that the science of handling pig iron is so great and amounts to so much that it is impossible for the man who is best suited to this type of work to understand the principles of this science, or even to work in accordance with these principles without the aid of a man better educated than he is. And the further illustrations to be given will make it clear that in almost all of the mechanic arts the science which underlies each workman's act is so great and amounts to so much that the workman who is best suited actually to do the work is incapable (either through lack of education or through insufficient mental capacity) of understanding this science. This is announced as a general principle, the truth of which will become apparent as one illustration after another is given. After showing these four elements in the handling of pig iron, several illustrations will be given of their application to different kinds of work in the field of the mechanic arts, at intervals in a rising scale, beginning with the simplest and ending with the more intricate forms of labor.

One of the first pieces of work undertaken by us, when the writer started to introduce scientific management into the Bethlehem Steel Company, was to handle pig iron on task work. The opening of the Spanish War found some 80,000 tons of pig iron placed in small piles in an open field adjoining the works. Prices for pig iron had been so low that it could not be sold at a profit, and it therefore had been stored. With the opening of the Spanish War the price of pig iron rose, and this large accumulation of iron was sold. This gave us a good opportunity to show the workmen, as well as the owners and managers of the works, on a fairly large scale the advantages of task work over the old-fashioned day work and piece work, in doing a very elementary class of work. The Bethlehem Steel Company had five blast furnaces, the product of which had been handled by a pig-iron gang for many years. This gang, at this time, consisted of about 75 men. They were good, average pig-iron handlers, were under an excellent foreman who himself had been a pig-iron handler, and the work was done, on the whole, about as fast and as cheaply as it was anywhere else at that time. A railroad switch was run out into the field, right along the edge of the piles of pig iron. An inclined plank was placed against the side of a car, and each man picked up from his pile a pig of iron weighing about 92 pounds, walked up the inclined plank and dropped it on the end of the car.

We found that this gang were loading on the average about 1212 long tons per man per day. We were surprised to find, after studying the matter, that a first-class pig-iron handler ought to handle between 47 and 48 long tons per day, instead of 1212 tons. This task seemed to us so very large that we were obliged to go over our work several times before we were absolutely sure that we were right. Once we were sure, however, that 47 tons was a proper day's work for a first-class pig-iron handler, the task which faced us as managers under the modern scientific plan was clearly before us. It was our duty to see that the 80,000 tons of pig iron was loaded on to the cars at the rate of 47 tons per man per day, in place of 1212 tons, at which rate the work was then being done. And it was further our duty to see that this work was done without bringing on a strike among the men, without any quarrel with the men, and to see that the men were happier and better contented when loading at the new rate of 47 tons than they were when loading at the old rate of 1212 tons.

Our first step was the scientific selection of the workman. In dealing with workmen under this type of management, it is an inflexible rule to talk to and deal with only one man at a time, since each workman has his own special abilities and limitations, and since we are not dealing with men in masses, but are trying to develop each individual man to his highest state of efficiency and prosperity. Our first step was to find the proper workman to begin with. We therefore carefully watched and studied these 75 men for three or four days, at the end of which time we had picked out four men who appeared to be physically able to handle pig iron at the rate of 47 tons per day. A careful study was then made of each of these men. We looked up their history as far back as practicable and thorough inquiries were made as to the character, habits, and the ambition of each of them. Finally we selected one from among the four as the most likely man to start with. He was a little Pennsylvania Dutchman who had been observed to trot back home for a mile or so after his work in the evening, about as fresh as he was when he came trotting down to work in the morning. We found that upon wages of $1.15 a day he had succeeded in buying a small plot of ground, and that he was engaged in putting up the walls of a little house for himself in the morning before starting to work and at night after leaving. He also had the reputation of being exceedingly "close," that is, of placing a very high value on a dollar. As one man whom we talked to about him said, "A penny looks about the size of a cart-wheel to him." This man we will call Schmidt. The task before us, then, narrowed itself down to getting Schmidt to handle 47 tons of pig iron per day and making him glad to do it. This was done as follows. Schmidt was called out from among the gang of pig-iron handlers and talked to somewhat in this way:

"Schmidt, are you a high-priced man?"

"Vell, I don't know vat you mean."

"Oh yes, you do. What I want to know is whether you are a high-priced man or not."

"Vell, I don't know vat you mean."

"Oh, come now, you answer my questions. What I want to find out is whether you are a high-priced man or one of these cheap fellows here. What I want to find out is whether you want to earn $1.85 a day or whether you are satisfied with $1.15, just the same as all those cheap fellows are getting."

"Did I vant $1.85 a day? Vas dot a high-priced man? Vell, yes, I vas a high-priced man."

"Oh, you're aggravating me. Of course you want $1.85 a day – every one wants it! You know perfectly well that that has very little to do with your being a high-priced man. For goodness' sake answer my questions, and don't waste any more of my time. Now come over here. You see that pile of pig iron?"

"Yes."

"You see that car?"

"Yes."

"Well, if you are a high-priced man, you will load that pig iron on that car to-morrow for $1.85. Now do wake up and answer my question. Tell me whether you are a high-priced man or not."

"Vell – did I got $1.85 for loading dot pig iron on dot car to-morrow?"

"Yes, of course you do, and you get $1.85 for loading a pile like that every day right through the year. That is what a high-priced man does, and you know it just as well as I do."

"Vell, dot's all right. I could load dot pig iron on the car to-morrow for $1.85, and I get it every day, don't I?"

"Certainly you do – certainly you do."

"Vell, den, I vas a high-priced man."

"Now, hold on, hold on. You know just as well as I do that a high-priced man has to do exactly as he's told from morning till night. You have seen this man here before, haven't you?"

"No, I never saw him."

"Well, if you are a high-priced man, you will do exactly as this man tells you to-morrow, from morning till night. When he tells you to pick up a pig and walk, you pick it up and you walk, and when he tells you to sit down and rest, you sit down. You do that right straight through the day. And what's more, no back talk. Now a high-priced man does just what he's told to do, and no back talk. Do you understand that? When this man tells you to walk, you walk; when he tells you to sit down, you sit down, and you don't talk back at him. Now you come on to work here to-morrow morning and I'll know before night whether you are really a high-priced man or not."

This seems to be rather rough talk. And indeed it would be if applied to an educated mechanic, or even an intelligent laborer. With a man of the mentally sluggish type of Schmidt it is appropriate and not unkind, since it is effective in fixing his attention on the high wages which he wants and away from what, if it were called to his attention, he probably would consider impossibly hard work. What would Schmidt's answer be if he were talked to in a manner which is usual under the management of "initiative and incentive"? say, as follows: "Now, Schmidt, you are a first-class pig-iron handler and know your business well. You have been handling at the rate of 1212 tons per day. I have given considerable study to handling pig iron, and feel sure that you could do a much larger day's work than you have been doing. Now don't you think that if you really tried you could handle 47 tons of pig iron per day, instead of 1212 tons?"

What do you think Schmidt's answer would be to this?

Schmidt started to work, and all day long, and at regular intervals, was told by the man who stood over him with a watch, "Now pick up a pig and walk. Now sit down and rest. Now walk – now rest," etc. He worked when he was told to work, and rested when he was told to rest, and at half-past five in the afternoon had his 4712 tons loaded on the car. And he practically never failed to work at this pace and do the task that was set him during the three years that the writer was at Bethlehem. And throughout this time he averaged a little more than $1.85 per day, whereas before he had never received over $1.15 per day, which was the ruling rate of wages at that time in Bethlehem. That is, he received 60 per cent. higher wages than were paid to other men who were not working on task work. One man after another was picked out and trained to handle pig iron at the rate of 4712 tons per day until all of the pig iron was handled at this rate, and the men were receiving 60 per cent. more wages than other workmen around them.

The writer has given above a brief description of three of the four elements which constitute the essence of scientific management: first, the careful selection of the workman, and, second and third, the method of first inducing and then training and helping the workman to work according to the scientific method. Nothing has as yet been said about the science of handling pig iron. The writer trusts, however, that before leaving this illustration the reader will be thoroughly convinced that there is a science of handling pig iron, and further that this science amounts to so much that the man who is suited to handle pig iron cannot possibly understand it, nor even work in accordance with the laws of this science, without the help of those who are over him.

The writer came into the machine-shop of the Midvale Steel Company in 1878, after having served an apprenticeship as a pattern-maker and as a machinist. This was close to the end of the long period of depression following the panic of 1873, and business was so poor that it was impossible for many mechanics to get work at their trades. For this reason he was obliged to start as a day laborer instead of working as a mechanic. Fortunately for him, soon after he came into the shop the clerk of the shop was found stealing. There was no one else available, and so, having more education than the other laborers (since he had been prepared for college) he was given the position of clerk. Shortly after this he was given work as a machinist in running one of the lathes, and, as he turned out rather more work than other machinists were doing on similar lathes, after several months was made gang-boss over the lathes.

Almost all of the work of this shop had been done on piece work for several years. As was usual then, and in fact as is still usual in most of the shops in this country, the shop was really run by the workmen, and not by the bosses. The workmen together had carefully planned just how fast each job should be done, and they had set a pace for each machine throughout the shop, which was limited to about one-third of a good day's work. Every new workman who came into the shop was told at once by the other men exactly how much of each kind of work he was to do, and unless he obeyed these instructions he was sure before long to be driven out of the place by the men.

As soon as the writer was made gang-boss, one after another of the men came to him and talked somewhat as follows: "Now, Fred, we're very glad to see that you've been made gang-boss. You know the game all right, and we're sure that you're not likely to be a piece-work hog. You come along with us, and everything will be all right, but if you try breaking any of these rates you can be mighty sure that we'll throw you over the fence."

The writer told them plainly that he was now working on the side of the management, and that he proposed to do whatever he could to get a fair day's work out of the lathes. This immediately started a war; in most cases a friendly war, because the men who were under him were his personal friends, but none the less a war, which as time went on grew more and more bitter. The writer used every expedient to make them do a fair day's work, such as discharging or lowering the wages of the more stubborn men who refused to make any improvement, and such as lowering the piece-work price, hiring green men, and personally teaching them how to do the work, with the promise from them that when they had learned how, they would then do a fair day's work. While the men constantly brought such pressure to bear (both inside and outside the works) upon all those who started to increase their output that they were finally compelled to do about as the rest did, or else quit. No one who has not had this experience can have an idea of the bitterness which is gradually developed in such a struggle. In a war of this kind the workmen have one expedient which is usually effective. They use their ingenuity to contrive various ways in which the machines which they are running are broken or damaged – apparently by accident, or in the regular course of work – and this they always lay at the door of the foreman, who has forced them to drive the machine so hard that it is overstrained and is being ruined. And there are few foremen indeed who are able to stand up against the combined pressure of all of the men in the shop. In this case the problem was complicated by the fact that the shop ran both day and night.

The writer had two advantages, however, which are not possessed by the ordinary foreman, and these came, curiously enough, from the fact that he was not the son of a working man.

First, owing to the fact that he happened not to be of working parents, the owners of the company believed that he had the interest of the works more at heart than the other workmen, and they therefore had more confidence in his word than they did in that of the machinists who were under him. So that, when the machinists reported to the Superintendent that the machines were being smashed up because an incompetent foreman was overstraining them, the Superintendent accepted the word of the writer when he said that these men were deliberately breaking their machines as a part of the piece-work war which was going on, and he also allowed the writer to make the only effective answer to this Vandalism on the part of the men, namely: "There will be no more accidents to the machines in this shop. If any part of a machine is broken the man in charge of it must pay at least a part of the cost of its repair, and the fines collected in this way will all be handed over to the mutual beneficial association to help care for sick workmen." This soon stopped the wilful breaking of machines.

Second. If the writer had been one of the workmen, and had lived where they lived, they would have brought such social pressure to bear upon him that it would have been impossible to have stood out against them. He would have been called "scab" and other foul names every time he appeared on the street, his wife would have been abused, and his children would have been stoned. Once or twice he was begged by some of his friends among the workmen not to walk home, about two and a half miles along the lonely path by the side of the railway. He was told that if he continued to do this it would be at the risk of his life. In all such cases, however, a display of timidity is apt to increase rather than diminish the risk, so the writer told these men to say to the other men in the shop that he proposed to walk home every night right up that railway track; that he never had carried and never would carry any weapon of any kind, and that they could shoot and be d——.

After about three years of this kind of struggling, the output of the machines had been materially increased, in many cases doubled, and as a result the writer had been promoted from one gang-boss-ship to another until he became foreman of the shop. For any right-minded man, however, this success is in no sense a recompense for the bitter relations which he is forced to maintain with all of those around him. Life which is one continuous struggle with other men is hardly worth living. His workman friends came to him continually and asked him, in a personal, friendly way, whether he would advise them, for their own best interest, to turn out more work. And, as a truthful man, he had to tell them that if he were in their place he would fight against turning out any more work, just as they were doing, because under the piece-work system they would be allowed to earn no more wages than they had been earning, and yet they would be made to work harder. Soon after being made foreman, therefore, he decided to make a determined effort to in some way change the system of management, so that the interests of the workmen and the management should become the same, instead of antagonistic. This resulted, some three years later, in the starting of the type of management which is described in papers presented to the American Society of Mechanical Engineers entitled "A Piece-Rate System" and "Shop Management."

In preparation for this system the writer realized that the greatest obstacle to harmonious cooperation between the workmen and the management lay in the ignorance of the management as to what really constitutes a proper day's work for a workman. He fully realized that, although he was foreman of the shop, the combined knowledge and skill of the workmen who were under him was certainly ten times as great as his own. He therefore obtained the permission of Mr. William Sellers, who was at that time the President of the Midvale Steel Company, to spend some money in a careful, scientific study of the time required to do various kinds of work.

Mr. Sellers allowed this more as a reward for having, to a certain extent, "made good" as foreman of the shop in getting more work out of the men, than for any other reason. He stated, however, that he did not believe that any scientific study of this sort would give results of much value.

Among several investigations which were undertaken at this time, one was an attempt to find some rule, or law, which would enable a foreman to know in advance how much of any kind of heavy laboring work a man who was well suited to his job ought to do in a day; that is, to study the tiring effect of heavy labor upon a first-class man. Our first step was to employ a young college graduate to look up all that had been written on the subject in English, German, and French. Two classes of experiments had been made: one by physiologists who were studying the endurance of the human animal, and the other by engineers who wished to determine what fraction of a horse-power a man-power was. These experiments had been made largely upon men who were lifting loads by means of turning the crank of a winch from which weights were suspended, and others who were engaged in walking, running, and lifting weights in various ways. However, the records of these investigations were so meager that no law of any value could be deduced from them. We therefore started a series of experiments of our own.

Two first-class laborers were selected, men who had proved themselves to be physically powerful and who were also good steady workers. These men were paid double wages during the experiments, and were told that they must work to the best of their ability at all times, and that we should make certain tests with them from time to time to find whether they were "soldiering" or not, and that the moment either one of them started to try to deceive us he would be discharged. They worked to the best of their ability throughout the time that they were being observed.

Now it must be clearly understood that in these experiments we were not trying to find the maximum work that a man could do on a short spurt or for a few days, but that our endeavor was to learn what really constituted a full day^s work for a first-class man; the best day^s work that a man could properly do, year in and year out, and still thrive under. These men were given all kinds of tasks, which were carried out each day under the close observation of the young college man who was conducting the experiments, and who at the same time noted with a stop-watch the proper time for all of the motions that were made by the men. Every element in any way connected with the work which we believed could have a bearing on the result was carefully studied and recorded. What we hoped ultimately to determine was what fraction of a horse-power a man was able to exert, that is, how many foot-pounds of work a man could do in a day.

After completing this series of experiments, therefore, each man^s work for each day was translated into foot-pounds of energy, and to our surprise we found that there was no constant or uniform relation between the foot-pounds of energy which the man exerted during a day and the tiring effect of his work. On some kinds of work the man would be tired out when doing perhaps not more than one-eighth of a horse-power, while in others he would be tired to no greater extent by doing half a horse-power of work. We failed, therefore, to find any law which was an accurate guide to the maximum day's work for a first-class workman. A large amount of very valuable data had been obtained, which enabled us to know, for many kinds of labor, what was a proper day^s work. It did not seem wise, however, at this time to spend any more money in trying to find the exact law which we were after. Some years later, when more money was available for this purpose, a second series of experiments was made, similar to the first, but somewhat more thorough. This, however, resulted as the first experiments, in obtaining valuable information but not in the development of a law. Again, some years later, a third series of experiments was made, and this time no trouble was spared in our endeavor to make the work thorough. Every minute element which could in any way affect the problem was carefully noted and studied, and two college men devoted about three months to the experiments. After this data was again translated into foot-pounds of energy exerted for each man each day, it became perfectly clear that there is no direct relation between the horse-power which a man exerts (that is, his foot-pounds of energy per day) and the tiring effect of the work on the man. The writer, however, was quite as firmly convinced as ever that some definite, clear-cut law existed as to what constitutes a full day^s work for a first-class laborer, and our data had been so carefully collected and recorded that he felt sure that the necessary information was included somewhere in the records. The problem of developing this law from the accumulated facts was therefore handed over to Mr. Carl G. Barth, who is a better mathematician than any of the rest of us, and we decided to investigate the problem in a new way, by graphically representing each element of the work through plotting curves, which should give us, as it were, a bird's-eye view of every element. In a comparatively short time Mr. Barth had discovered the law governing the tiring effect of heavy labor on a first-class man. And it is so simple in its nature that it is truly remarkable that it should not have been discovered and clearly understood years before. The law which was developed is as follows:

The law is confined to that class of work in which the limit of a man's capacity is reached because he is tired out. It is the law of heavy laboring, corresponding to the work of the cart horse, rather than that of the trotter. Practically all such work consists of a heavy pull or a push on the man's arms, that is, the man's strength is exerted by either lifting or pushing something which he grasps in his hands. And the law is that for each given pull or push on the man's arms it is possible for the workman to be under load for only a definite percentage of the day. For example, when pig iron is being handled (each pig weighing 92 pounds), a first-class workman can only be under load 43 per cent. of the day. He must be entirely free from load during 57 per cent. of the day. And as the load becomes lighter, the percentage of the day under which the man can remain under load increases. So that, if the workman is handling a half-pig, weighing 46 pounds, he can then be under load 58 per cent. of the day, and only has to rest during 42 per cent. As the weight grows lighter the man can remain under load during a larger and larger percentage of the day, until finally a load is reached which he can carry in his hands all day long without being tired out. When that point has been arrived at this law ceases to be useful as a guide to a laborer's endurance, and some other law must be found which indicates the man's capacity for work.

When a laborer is carrying a piece of pig iron weighing 92 pounds in his hands, it tires him about as much to stand still under the load as it does to walk with it, since his arm muscles are under the same severe tension whether he is moving or not. A man, however, who stands still under a load is exerting no horse-power whatever, and this accounts for the fact that no constant relation could be traced in various kinds of heavy laboring work between the foot-pounds of energy exerted and the tiring effect of the work on the man. It will also be clear that in all work of this kind it is necessary for the arms of the workman to be completely free from load (that is, for the workman to rest) at frequent intervals. Throughout the time that the man is under a heavy load the tissues of his arm muscles are in process of degeneration, and frequent periods of rest are required in order that the blood may have a chance to restore these tissues to their normal condition.

To return now to our pig-iron handlers at the Bethlehem Steel Company. If Schmidt had been allowed to attack the pile of 47 tons of pig iron without the guidance or direction of a man who understood the art, or science, of handling pig iron, in his desire to earn his high wages he would probably have tired himself out by 11 or 12 o'clock in the day. He would have kept so steadily at work that his muscles would not have had the proper periods of rest absolutely needed for recuperation, and he would have been completely exhausted early in the day. By having a man, however, who understood this law, stand over him and direct his work, day after day, until he acquired the habit of resting at proper intervals, he was able to work at an even gait all day long without unduly tiring himself.

Now one of the very first requirements for a man who is fit to handle pig iron as a regular occupation is that he shall be so stupid and so phlegmatic that he more nearly resembles in his mental make-up the ox than any other type. The man who is mentally alert and intelligent is for this very reason entirely unsuited to what would, for him, be the grinding monotony of work of this character. Therefore the workman who is best suited to handling pig iron is unable to understand the real science of doing this class of work. He is so stupid that the word "percentage" has no meaning to him, and he must consequently be trained by a man more intelligent than himself into the habit of working in accordance with the laws of this science before he can be successful.

The writer trusts that it is now clear that even in the case of the most elementary form of labor that is known, there is a science, and that when the man best suited to this class of work has been carefully selected, when the science of doing the work has been developed, and when the carefully selected man has been trained to work in accordance with this science, the results obtained must of necessity be overwhelmingly greater than those which are possible under the plan of 'initiative and incentive."

Let us, however, again turn to the case of these pig-iron handlers, and see whether, under the ordinary type of management, it would not have been possible to obtain practically the same results. The writer has put the problem before many good managers, and asked them whether, under premium work, piece work, or any of the ordinary plans of management, they would be likely even to approximate 47 tons per man per day, and not a man has suggested that an output of over 18 to 25 tons could be attained by any of the ordinary expedients. It will be remembered that the Bethlehem men were loading only 12½ tons per man. To go into the matter in more detail, however: As to the scientific selection of the men, it is a fact that in this gang of 75 pig-iron handlers only about one man in eight was physically capable of handling 47½ tons per day. With the very best of intentions, the other seven out of eight men were physically unable to work at this pace. Now the one man in eight who was able to do this work was in no sense superior to the other men who were working on the gang. He merely happened to be a man of the type of the ox, – no rare specimen of humanity, difficult to find and therefore very highly prized. On the contrary, he was a man so stupid that he was unfitted to do most kinds of laboring work, even. The selection of the man, then, does not involve finding some extraordinary individual, but merely picking out from among very ordinary men the few who are especially suited to this type of work. Although in this particular gang only one man in eight was suited to doing the work, we had not the slightest difficulty in getting all the men who were needed – some of them from inside of the works and others from the neighboring country – who were exactly suited to the job.

Under the management of "initiative and incentive" the attitude of the management is that of "putting the work up to the workmen." What likelihood would there be, then, under the old type of management, of these men properly selecting themselves for pig-iron handling? Would they be likely to get rid of seven men out of eight from their own gang and retain only the eighth man? No! And no expedient could be devised which would make these men properly select themselves. Even if they fully realized the necessity of doing so in order to obtain high wages (and they are not sufficiently intelligent properly to grasp this necessity), the fact that their friends or their brothers who were working right alongside of them would temporarily be thrown out of a job because they were not suited to this kind of work would entirely prevent them from properly selecting themselves, that is, from removing the seven out of eight men on the gang who were unsuited to pig-iron handling.

As to the possibility, under the old type of management, of inducing these pig-iron handlers (after they had been properly selected) to work in accordance with the science of doing heavy laboring, namely, having proper scientifically determined periods of rest in close sequence to periods of work. As has been indicated before, the essential idea of the ordinary types of management is that each workman has become more skilled in his own trade than it is possible for any one in the management to be, and that, therefore, the details of how the work shall best be done must be left to him. The idea, then, of taking one man after another and training him under a competent teacher into new working habits until he continually and habitually works in accordance with scientific laws, which have been developed by some one else, is directly antagonistic to the old idea that each workman can best regulate his own way of doing the work. And besides this, the man suited to handling pig iron is too stupid properly to train himself. Thus it will be seen that with the ordinary types of management the development of scientific knowledge to replace rule of thumb, the scientific selection of the men, and inducing the men to work in accordance with these scientific principles are entirely out of the question. And this because the philosophy of the old management puts the entire responsibility upon the workmen, while the philosophy of the new places a great part of it upon the management.

With most readers great sympathy will be aroused because seven out of eight of these pig-iron handlers were thrown out of a job. This sympathy is entirely wasted, because almost all of them were immediately given other jobs with the Bethlehem Steel Company. And indeed it should be understood that the removal of these men from pig-iron handling, for which they were unfit, was really a kindness to themselves, because it was the first step toward finding them work for which they were peculiarly fitted, and at which, after receiving proper training, they could permanently and legitimately earn higher wages. Although the reader may be convinced that there is a certain science back of the handling of pig iron, still it is more than likely that he is still skeptical as to the existence of a science for doing other kinds of laboring. One of the important objects of this paper is to convince its readers that every single act of every workman can be reduced to a science. With the hope of fully convincing the reader of this fact, therefore, the writer proposes to give several more simple illustrations from among the thousands which are at hand.

For example, the average man would question whether there is much of any science in the work of shoveling. Yet there is but little doubt, if any intelligent reader of this paper were deliberately to set out to find what may be called the foundation of the science of shoveling, that with perhaps 15 to 20 hours of thought and analysis he would be almost sure to have arrived at the essence of this science. On the other hand, so completely are the rule-of-thumb ideas still dominant that the writer has never met a single shovel contractor to whom it had ever even occurred that there was such a thing as the science of shoveling. This science is so elementary as to be almost self-evident.

For a first-class shoveler there is a given shovel load at which he will do his biggest day's work. What is this shovel load? Will a first-class man do more work per day with a shovel load of 5 pounds, 10 pounds, 15 pounds, 20, 25, 30, or 40 pounds? Now this is a question which can be answered only through carefully made experiments. By first selecting two or three first-class shovelers, and paying them extra wages for doing trustworthy work, and then gradually varying the shovel load and having all the conditions accompanying the work carefully observed for several weeks by men who were used to experimenting, it was found that a first-class man would do his biggest day's work with a shovel load of about 21 pounds. For instance, that this man would shovel a larger tonnage per day with a 21- pound load than with a 24-pound load or than with an 18-pound load on his shovel. It is, of course, evident that no shoveler can always take a load of exactly 21 pounds on his shovel, but nevertheless, although his load may vary 3 or 4 pounds one way or the other, either below or above the 21 pounds, he will do his biggest day's work when his average for the day is about 21 pounds.

The writer does not wish it to be understood that this is the whole of the art or science of shoveling. There are many other elements, which together go to make up this science. But he wishes to indicate the important effect which this one piece of scientific knowledge has upon the work of shoveling.

At the works of the Bethlehem Steel Company, for example, as a result of this law, instead of allowing each shoveler to select and own his own shovel, it became necessary to provide some 8 to 10 different kinds of shovels, etc., each one appropriate to handling a given type of material; not only so as to enable the men to handle an average load of 21 pounds, but also to adapt the shovel to several other requirements which become perfectly evident when this work is studied as a science. A large shovel tool room was built, in which were stored not only shovels but carefully designed and standardized labor implements of all kinds, such as picks, crowbars, etc. This made it possible to issue to each workman a shovel which would hold a load of 21 pounds of whatever class of material they were to handle: a small shovel for ore, say, or a large one for ashes. Iron ore is one of the heavy materials which are handled in a works of this kind, and rice coal, owing to the fact that it is so slippery on the shovel, is one of the lightest materials. And it was found on studying the rule-of-thumb plan at the Bethlehem Steel Company, where each shoveler owned his own shovel, that he would frequently go from shoveling ore, with a load of about 30 pounds per shovel, to handling rice coal, with a load on the same shovel of less than 4 pounds. In the one case, he was so overloaded that it was impossible for him to do a full day's work, and in the other case he was so ridiculously underloaded that it was manifestly impossible to even approximate a day's work.

Briefly to illustrate some of the other elements which go to make up the science of shoveling, thousands of stop-watch observations were made to study just how quickly a laborer, provided in each case with the proper type of shovel, can push his shovel into the pile of materials and then draw it out properly loaded. These observations were made first when pushing the shovel into the body of the pile. Next when shoveling on a dirt bottom, that is, at the outside edge of the pile, and next with a wooden bottom, and finally with an iron bottom. Again a similar accurate time study was made of the time required to swing the shovel backward and then throw the load for a given horizontal distance, accompanied by a given height. This time study was made for various combinations of distance and height. With data of this sort before him, coupled with the law of endurance described in the case of the pig-iron handlers, it is evident that the man who is directing shovelers can first teach them the exact methods which should be employed to use their strength to the very best advantage, and can then assign them daily tasks which are so just that the workman can each day be sure of earning the large bonus which is paid whenever he successfully performs this task.

There were about 600 shovelers and laborers of this general class in the yard of the Bethlehem Steel Company at this time. These men were scattered in their work over a yard which was, roughly, about two miles long and half a mile wide. In order that each workman should be given his proper implement and his proper instructions for doing each new job, it was necessary to establish a detailed system for directing men in their work, in place of the old plan of handling them in large groups, or gangs, under a few yard foremen. As each workman came into the works in the morning, he took out of his own special pigeonhole, with his number on the outside, two pieces of paper, one of which stated just what implements he was to get from the tool room and where he was to start to work, and the second of which gave the history of his previous day's work; that is, a statement of the work which he had done, how much he had earned the day before, etc. Many of these men were foreigners and unable to read and write, but they all knew at a glance the essence of this report, because yellow paper showed the man that he had failed to do his full task the day before, and informed him that he had not earned as much as $1.85 a day, and that none but high-priced men would be allowed to stay permanently with this gang. The hope was further expressed that he would earn his full wages on the following day. So that whenever the men received white slips they knew that everything was all right, and whenever they received yellow slips they realized that they must do better or they would be shifted to some other class of work.

Dealing with every workman as a separate individual in this way involved the building of a labor office for the superintendent and clerks who were in charge of this section of the work. In this office every laborer's work was planned out well in advance, and the workmen were all moved from place to place by the clerks with elaborate diagrams or maps of the yard before them, very much as chessmen are moved on a chess-board, a telephone and messenger system having been installed for this purpose. In this way a large amount of the time lost through having too many men in one place and too few in another, and through waiting between jobs, was entirely eliminated. Under the old system the workmen were kept day after day in comparatively large gangs, each under a single foreman, and the gang was apt to remain of pretty nearly the same size whether there was much or little of the particular kind of work on hand which this foreman had under his charge, since each gang had to be kept large enough to handle whatever work in its special line was likely to come along.

When one ceases to deal with men in large gangs or groups, and proceeds to study each workman as an individual, if the workman fails to do his task, some competent teacher should be sent to show him exactly how his work can best be done, to guide, help, and encourage him, and, at the same time, to study his possibilities as a workman. So that, under the plan which individualizes each workman, instead of brutally discharging the man or lowering his wages for failing to make good at once, he is given the time and the help required to make him proficient at his present job, or he is shifted to another class of work for which he is either mentally or physically better suited.

All of this requires the kindly cooperation of the management, and involves a much more elaborate organization and system than the old-fashioned herding of men in large gangs. This organization consisted, in this case, of one set of men, who were engaged in the development of the science of laboring through time study, such as has been described above; another set of men, mostly skilled laborers themselves, who were teachers, and who helped and guided the men in their work; another set of tool-room men who provided them with the proper implements and kept them in perfect order, and another set of clerks who planned the work well in advance, moved the men with the least loss of time from one place to another, and properly recorded each man's earnings, etc. And this furnishes an elementary illustration of what has been referred to as cooperation between the management and the workmen.

The question which naturally presents itself is whether an elaborate organization of this sort can be made to pay for itself; whether such an organization is not top-heavy. This question will best be answered by a statement of the results of the third year of working under this plan.

	Old Plan	*New Plan Task Work*
The number of yard laborers was reduced from between	400 & 600 down to about	140
Average number of tons per man per day	16	59
Average earnings per man per day	$1.15	$1.88
Average cost of handling a ton of 2240 lbs	$0.072	$0.033

And in computing the low cost of $0.033 per ton, the office and tool-room expenses, and the wages of all labor superintendents, foremen, clerks, time-study men, etc., are included.

During this year the total saving of the new plan over the old amounted to $36,417.69, and during the six months following, when all of the work of the yard was on task work, the saving was at the rate of between $75,000 and $80,000 per year.

Perhaps the most important of all the results attained was the effect on the workmen themselves. A careful inquiry into the condition of these men developed the fact that out of the 140 workmen only two were said to be drinking men. This does not, of course, imply that many of them did not take an occasional drink. The fact is that a steady drinker would find it almost impossible to keep up with the pace which was set, so that they were practically all sober. Many, if not most of them, were saving money, and they all lived better than they had before. These men constituted the finest body of picked laborers that the writer has ever seen together, and they looked upon the men who were over them, their bosses and their teachers, as their very best friends; not as nigger drivers, forcing them to work extra hard for ordinary wages, but as friends who were teaching them and helping them to earn much higher wages than they had ever earned before. It would have been absolutely impossible for any one to have stirred up strife between these men and their employers.

And this presents a very simple though effective illustration of what is meant by the words "prosperity for the employé, coupled with prosperity for the employer," the two principal objects of management. It is evident also that this result has been brought about by the application of the four fundamental principles of scientific management.

As another illustration of the value of a scientific study of the motives which influence workmen in their daily work, the loss of ambition and initiative will be cited, which takes place in workmen when they are herded into gangs instead of being treated as separate individuals. A careful analysis had demonstrated the fact that when workmen are herded together in gangs, each man in the gang becomes far less efficient than when his personal ambition is stimulated; that when men work in gangs, their individual efficiency falls almost invariably down to or below the level of the worst man in the gang; and that they are all pulled down instead of being elevated by being herded together. For this reason a general order had been issued in the Bethlehem Steel Works that not more than four men were to be allowed to work in a labor gang without a special permit, signed by the General Superintendent of the works, this special permit to extend for one week only. It was arranged that as far as possible each laborer should be given a separate individual task. As there were about 5000 men at work in the establishment, the General Superintendent had so much to do that there was but little time left for signing these special permits.

After gang work had been by this means broken up, an unusually fine set of ore shovelers had been developed, through careful selection and individual, scientific training. Each of these men was given a separate car to unload each day, and his wages depended upon his own personal work. The man who unloaded the largest amount of ore was paid the highest wages, and an unusual opportunity came for demonstrating the importance of individualizing each workman. Much of this ore came from the Lake Superior region, and the same ore was delivered both in Pittsburg and in Bethlehem in exactly similar cars. There was a shortage of ore handlers in Pittsburg, and hearing of the fine gang of laborers that had been developed at Bethlehem, one of the Pittsburg steel works sent an agent to hire the Bethlehem men. The Pittsburg men offered 4910 cents a ton for unloading exactly the same ore, with the same shovels, from the same cars, that were unloaded in Bethlehem for 3210 cents a ton. After carefully considering this situation, it was decided that it would be unwise to pay more than 3210 cents per ton for unloading the Bethlehem cars, because, at this rate, the Bethlehem laborers were earning a little over $1.85 per man per day, and this price was 60 per cent, more than the ruling rate of wages around Bethlehem.

A long series of experiments, coupled with close observation, had demonstrated the fact that when workmen of this caliber are given a carefully measured task, which calls for a big day's work on their part, and that when in return for this extra effort they are paid wages up to 60 per cent, beyond the wages usually paid, that this increase in wages tends to make them not only more thrifty but better men in every way; that they live rather better, begin to save money, become more sober, and work more steadily. When, on the ether hand, they receive much more than a 60 per cent, increase in wages, many of them will work irregularly and tend to become more or less shiftless, extravagant, and dissipated. Our experiments showed, in other words, that it does not do for most men to get rich too fast.

After deciding, for this reason, not to raise the wages of our ore handlers, these men were brought into the office one at a time, and talked to somewhat as follows:

"Now, Patrick, you have proved to us that you are a high-priced man. You have been earning every day a little more than $1.85, and you are just the sort of man that we want to have in our ore-shoveling gang. A man has come here from Pittsburg, who is offering 4910 cents per ton for handling ore while we can pay only 3210 cents per ton. I think, therefore, that you had better apply to this man for a job. Of course, you know we are very sorry to have you leave us, but you have proved yourself a high-priced man, and we are very glad to see you get this chance of earning more money. Just remember, however, that at any time in the future, when you get out of a job, you can always come right back to us. There will always be a job for a high-priced man like you in our gang here."

Almost all of the ore handlers took this advice, and went to Pittsburg, but in about six weeks most of them were again back in Bethlehem unloading ore at the old rate of 3210 cents a ton. The writer had the following talk with one of these men after he had returned:

"Patrick, what are you doing back here? I thought we had gotten rid of you."

"Well, sir. I'll tell you how it was. When we got out there Jimmy and I were put on to a car with eight other men. We started to shovel the ore out just the same as we do here. After about half an hour I saw a little devil alongside of me doing pretty near nothing, so I said to him, 'Why don't you go to work? Unless we get the ore out of this car we won't get any money on pay-day.' He turned to me and said, 'Who in — are you?' 'Well,' I said, 'that's none of your business'; and the little devil stood up to me and said, 'You'll be minding your own business, or I'll throw you off this car!' 'Well, I could have spit on him and drowned him, but the rest of the men put down their shovels and looked as if they were going to back him up; so I went round to Jimmy and said (so that the whole gang could hear it), 'Now, Jimmy, you and I will throw a shovelful whenever this little devil throws one, and not another shovelful.' So we watched him, and only shoveled when he shoveled. – When pay-day came around, though, we had less money than we got here at Bethlehem. After that Jimmy and I went in to the boss, and asked him for a car to ourselves, the same as we got at Bethlehem, but he told us to mind our own business. And when another pay-day came around we had less money than we got here at Bethlehem, so Jimmy and I got the gang together and brought them all back here to work again."

When working each man for himself, these men were able to earn higher wages at 3210 cents a ton than they could earn when they were paid 4910 cents a ton on gang work; and this again shows the great gain which results from working according to even the most elementary of scientific principles. But it also shows that in the application of the most elementary principles it is necessary for the management to do their share of the work in cooperating with the workmen. The Pittsburg managers knew just how the results had been attained at Bethlehem, but they were unwilling to go to the small trouble and expense required to plan ahead and assign a separate car to each shoveler, and then keep an individual record of each man's work, and pay him just what he had earned.

Bricklaying is one of the oldest of our trades. For hundreds of years there has been little or no improvement made in the implements and materials used in this trade, nor in fact in the method of laying bricks. In spite of the millions of men who have practised this trade, no great improvement has been evolved for many generations. Here, then, at least, one would expect to find but little gain possible through scientific analysis and study. Mr. Frank B. Gilbreth, a member of our Society, who had himself studied bricklaying in his youth, became interested in the principles of scientific management, and decided to apply them to the art of bricklaying. He made an intensely interesting analysis and study of each movement of the bricklayer, and one after another eliminated all unnecessary movements and substituted fast for slow motions. He experimented with every minute element which in any way affects the speed and the tiring of the bricklayer.

He developed the exact position which each of the feet of the bricklayer should occupy with relation to the wall, the mortar box, and the pile of bricks, and so made it unnecessary for him to take a step or two toward the pile of bricks and back again each time a brick is laid.

He studied the best height for the mortar box and brick pile, and then designed a scaffold, with a table on it, upon which all of the materials are placed, so as to keep the bricks, the mortar, the man, and the wall in their proper relative positions. These scaffolds are adjusted, as the wall grows in height, for all of the bricklayers by a laborer especially detailed for this purpose, and by this means the bricklayer is saved the exertion of stooping down to the level of his feet for each brick and each trowelful of mortar and then straightening up again. Think of the waste of effort that has gone on through all these years, with each bricklayer lowering his body, weighing, say, 150 pounds, down two feet and raising it up again every time a brick (weighing about 5 pounds) is laid in the wall! And this each bricklayer did about one thousand times a day.

As a result of further study, after the bricks are unloaded from the cars, and before bringing them to the bricklayer, they are carefully sorted by a laborer, and placed with their best edge up on a simple wooden frame, constructed so as to enable him to take hold of each brick in the quickest time and in the most advantageous position. In this way the bricklayer avoids either having to turn the brick over or end for end to examine it before laying it, and he saves, also, the time taken in deciding which is the best edge and end to place on the outside of the wall. In most cases, also, he saves the time taken in disentangling the brick from a disorderly pile on the scaffold. This "pack" of bricks (as Mr. Gilbreth calls his loaded wooden frames) is placed by the helper in its proper position on the adjustable scaffold close to the mortar box.

We have all been used to seeing bricklayers tap each brick after it is placed on its bed of mortar several times with the end of the handle of the trowel so as to secure the right thickness for the joint. Mr. Gilbreth found that by tempering the mortar just right, the bricks could be readily bedded to the proper depth by a downward pressure of the hand with which they are laid. He insisted that his mortar mixers should give special attention to tempering the mortar, and so save the time consumed in tapping the brick.

Through all of this minute study of the motions to be made by the bricklayer in laying bricks under standard conditions, Mr. Gilbreth has reduced his movements from eighteen motions per brick to five, and even in one case to as low as two motions per brick. He has given all of the details of this analysis to the profession in the chapter headed "Motion Study," of his book entitled "Bricklaying System," published by Myron C. Clerk Publishing Company, New York and Chicago; E. F. N. Spon, of London.

An analysis of the expedients used by Mr. Gilbreth in reducing the motions of his bricklayers from eighteen to five shows that this improvement has been made in three different ways:

First. He has entirely dispensed with certain movements which the bricklayers in the past believed were necessary, but which a careful study and trial on his part have shown to be useless.

Second. He has introduced simple apparatus, such as his adjustable scaffold and his packets for holding the bricks, by means of which, with a very small amount of cooperation from a cheap laborer, he entirely eliminates a lot of tiresome and time-consuming motions which are necessary for the bricklayer who lacks the scaffold and the packet.

Third. He teaches his bricklayers to make simple motions with both hands at the same time, where before they completed a motion with the right hand and followed it later with one from the left hand.

For example, Mr. Gilbreth teaches his bricklayer to pick up a brick in the left hand at the same instant that he takes a trowelful of mortar with the right hand. This work with two hands at the same time is, of course, made possible by substituting a deep mortar box for the old mortar board (on which the mortar spread out so thin that a step or two had to be taken to reach it) and then placing the mortar box and the brick pile close together, and at the proper height on his new scaffold.

These three kinds of improvements are typical of the ways in which needless motions can be entirely eliminated and quicker types of movements substituted for slow movements when scientific motion study, as Mr. Gilbreth calls his analysis, time study, as the writer has called similar work, are applied in any trade.

Most practical men would (knowing the opposition of almost all tradesmen to making any change in their methods and habits), however, be skeptical as to the possibility of actually achieving any large results from a study of this sort. Mr. Gilbreth reports that a few months ago, in a large brick building which he erected, he demonstrated on a commercial scale the great gain which is possible from practically applying his scientific study. With union bricklayers, in laying a factory wall, twelve inches thick, with two kinds of brick, faced and ruled joints on both sides of the wall, he averaged, after his selected workmen had become skilful in his new methods, 350 bricks per man *per hour*; whereas the average speed of doing this work with the old methods was, in that section of the country, 120 bricks per man per hour. His bricklayers were taught his new method of bricklaying by their foreman. Those who failed to profit by their teaching were dropped, and each man as he became proficient under the new method, received a substantial (not a small) increase in his wages. With a view to individualizing his workmen and stimulating each man to do his best, Mr. Gilbreth also developed an ingenious method for measuring and recording the number of bricks laid by each man, and for telling each workman at frequent intervals how many bricks he had succeeded in laying.

It is only when this work is compared with the conditions which prevail under the tyranny of some of our misguided bricklayers' unions that the great waste of human effort which is going on will be realized. In one foreign city the bricklayers' union have restricted their men to *275 bricks per day* on work of this character when working for the city, and *375* per day when working for private owners. The members of this union are probably sincere in their belief that this restriction of output is a benefit to their trade, It should be plain to all men, however, that this deliberate loafing is almost criminal, in that it inevitably results in making every workman's family pay higher rent for their housing, and also in the end drives work and trade away from their city, instead of bringing it to it.

Why is it, in a trade which has been continually practised since before the Christian era, and with implements practically the same as they now are, that this simplification of the bricklayer's movements, this great gain, has not been made before?

It is highly likely that many times during all of these years individual bricklayers have recognized the possibility of eliminating each of these unnecessary motions. But even if, in the past, he did invent each one of Mr. Gilbreth's improvements, no bricklayer could alone increase his speed through their adoption because it will be remembered that in all cases several bricklayers work together in a row and that the walls all around a building must grow at the same rate of speed. No one bricklayer, then, can work much faster than the one next to him. Nor has any one workman the authority to make other men cooperate with him to do faster work. It is only through *enforced* standardization of methods, *enforced* adoption of the best implements and working conditions, and *enforced* cooperation that this faster work can be assured. And the duty of enforcing the adoption of standards and of enforcing this cooperation rests with the *management* alone. The *management* must supply continually one or more teachers to show each new man the new and simpler motions, and the slower men must be constantly watched and helped until they have risen to their proper speed. All of those who, after proper teaching, either will not or cannot work in accordance with the new methods and at the higher speed must be discharged by the management. The management must also recognize the broad fact that workmen will not submit to this more rigid standardization and will not work extra hard, unless they receive extra pay for doing it. All of this involves an individual study of and treatment for each man, while in the past they have been handled in large groups. The *management* must also see that those who prepare the bricks and the mortar and adjust the scaffold, etc., for the bricklayers, cooperate with them by doing their work just right and always on time; and they must also inform each bricklayer at frequent intervals as to the progress he is making, so that he may not unintentionally fall off in his pace. Thus it will be seen that it is the assumption by the management of new duties and new kinds of work never done by employers in the past that makes this great improvement possible, and that, without this new help from the management, the workman even with full knowledge of the new methods and with the best of intentions could not attain these startling results.

Mr. Gilbreth's method of bricklaying furnishes a simple illustration of true and effective cooperation. Not the type of cooperation in which a mass of workmen on one side together cooperate with the management; but that in which several men in the management (each one in his own particular way) help each workman individually, on the one hand, by studying his needs and his shortcomings and teaching him better and quicker methods, and, on the other hand, by seeing that all other workmen with whom he comes in contact help and cooperate with him by doing their part of the work right and fast.

The writer has gone thus fully into Mr. Gilbreth's method in order that it may be perfectly clear that this increase in output and that this harmony could not have been attained under the management of "initiative and incentive" (that is, by putting the problem up to the workman and leaving him to solve it alone) which has been the philosophy of the past. And that his success has been due to the use of the four elements which constitute the essence of scientific management.

First. The development (by the management, not the workman) of the science of bricklaying, with rigid rules for each motion of every man, and the perfection and standardization of all implements and working conditions.

Second. The careful selection and subsequent training of the bricklayers into first-class men, and the elimination of all men who refuse to or are unable to adopt the best methods.

Third. Bringing the first-class bricklayer and the science of bricklaying together, through the constant help and watchfulness of the management, and through paying each man a large daily bonus for working fast and doing what he is told to do.

Fourth. An almost equal division of the work and responsibility between the workman and the management. All day long the management work almost side by side with the men, helping, encouraging, and smoothing the way for them, while in the past they stood one side, gave the men but little help, and threw on to them almost the entire responsibility as to methods, implements, speed, and harmonious cooperation.

Of these four elements, the first (the development of the science of bricklaying) is the most interesting and spectacular. Each of the three others is, however, quite as necessary for success.

It must not be forgotten that back of all this, and directing it, there must be the optimistic, determined, and hard-working leader who can wait patiently as well as work.

In most cases (particularly when the work to be done is intricate in its nature) the "development of the science" is the most important of the four great elements of the new management. There are instances, however, in which the "scientific selection of the workman" counts for more than anything else. A case of this type is well illustrated in the very simple though unusual work of inspecting bicycle balls.

When the bicycle craze was at its height some years ago several million small balls made of hardened steel were used annually in bicycle bearings. And among the twenty or more operations used in making steel balls, perhaps the most important was that of inspecting them after final polishing so as to remove all fire-cracked or otherwise imperfect balls before boxing.

The writer was given the task of systematizing the largest bicycle ball factory in this country. This company had been running for from eight to ten years on ordinary day work before he undertook its reorganization, so that the one hundred and twenty or more girls who were inspecting the balls were "old hands" and skilled at their jobs. It is impossible even in the most elementary work to change rapidly from the old independence of individual day work to scientific cooperation. In most cases, however, there exist certain imperfections in working conditions which can at once be improved with benefit to all concerned.

In this instance it was found that the inspectors (girls) were working ten and one-half hours per day (with a Saturday half holiday.) Their work consisted briefly in placing a row of small polished steel balls on the back of the left hand, in the crease between two of the fingers pressed together, and while they were rolled over and over, they were minutely examined in a strong light, and with the aid of a magnet held in the right hand, the defective balls were picked out and thrown into especial boxes. Four kinds of defects were looked for – dented, soft, scratched, and fire-cracked – and they were mostly so minute as to be invisible to an eye not especially trained to this work. It required the closest attention and concentration, so that the nervous tension of the inspectors was considerable, in spite of the fact that they were comfortably seated and were not physically tired.

A most casual study made it evident that a very considerable part of the ten and one-half hours during which the girls were supposed to work was really spent in idleness because the working period was too long.

It is a matter of ordinary common sense to plan working hours so that the workers can really "work while they work" and "play while they play," and not mix the two.

Before the arrival of Mr. Sanford E. Thompson, who undertook a scientific study of the whole process, we decided, therefore, to shorten the working hours.

The old foreman who had been over the inspecting room for years was instructed to interview one after another of the better inspectors and the more influential girls and persuade them that they could do just as much work in ten hours each day as they had been doing in ten and one-half hours. Each girl was told that the proposition was to shorten the day's work to ten hours and pay them the same day's pay they were receiving for the ten and one-half hours.

In about two weeks the foreman reported that all of the girls he had talked to agreed that they could do their present work just as well in ten hours as in ten and one-half and that they approved of the change.

The writer had not been especially noted for his tact so he decided that it would be wise for him to display a little more of this quality by having the girls vote on the new proposition. This decision was hardly justified, however, for when the vote was taken the girls were unanimous that 1012 hours was good enough for them and they wanted no innovation of any kind.

This settled the matter for the time being. A few months later tact was thrown to the winds and the working hours were arbitrarily shortened in successive steps to 10 hours, 912, 9, and 812 (the pay per day remaining the same); and with each shortening of the working day the output increased instead of diminishing.

The change from the old to the scientific method in this department was made under the direction of Mr. Sanford E. Thompson, perhaps the most experienced man in motion and time study in this country, under the general superintendence of Mr. H. L. Gautt.

In the Physiological departments of our universities experiments are regularly conducted to determine what is known as the "personal coefficient" of the man tested. This is done by suddenly bringing some object, the letter *A* or *B* for instance, within the range of vision of the subject, who, the instant he recognizes the letter has to do some definite thing, such as to press a particular electric button. The time which elapses from the instant the letter comes in view until the subject presses the button is accurately recorded by a delicate scientific instrument.

This test show conclusively that there is a great difference in the "personal coefficient" of different men. Some individuals are born with unusually quick powers of perception accompanied by quick responsive action. With some the message is almost instantly transmitted from the eye to the brain, and the brain equally quickly responds by sending the proper message to the hand.

Men of this type are said to have a low "personal coefficient," while those of slow perception and slow action have a *high* "personal coefficient."

Mr. Thompson soon recognized that the quality most needed for a bicycle ball inspectors was a low "personal coefficient." Of course the ordinary qualities of endurance and industry were also called for.

For the ultimate good of the girls as well as the company, however, it became necessary to exclude all girls who lacked a low "personal coefficient." And unfortmiately this involved laying off many of the most intelligent, hardest working, and most trustworthy girls merely because they did not possess the quality of quick perception followed by quick action.

While the gradual selection of girls was going on other changes were also being made. One of the dangers to be guarded against, when the pay of the man or woman is made in any way to depend on the quantity of the work done, is that in the effort to increase the quantity the quality is apt to deteriorate.

It is necessary in almost all cases, therefore, to take definite steps to insure against any falling off in quality before moving in any way towards an increase in quantity.

In the work of these particular girls quality was the very essence. They were engaged in picking out all defective balls.

The first step, therefore, was to make it impossible for them to slight their work without being found out. This was accomplished through what is known as over-inspection. Each one of four of the most trustworthy girls was given each day a lot of balls to inspect which had been examined the day before by one of the regular inspectors; the number identifying the lot to be over-inspected having been changed by the foreman so that none of the over-inspectors knew whose work they were examining. In addition to this one of the lots inspected by the four over-inspectors was examined on the following day by the chief inspector, selected on account of her especial accuracy and integrity.

An effective expedient was adopted for checking the honesty and accuracy of the over-inspection. Every two or three days a lot of balls was especially prepared by the foreman, who counted out a definite number of perfect balls, and added a recorded number of defective balls of each kind. Neither the inspectors nor the over-inspectors had any means of distinguishing this prepared lot from the regular commercial lots. And in this way all temptation to slight their work or make false returns was removed.

After insuring in this way against deterioration in quality, effective means were at once adopted to increase the output. Improved day work was substituted for the old slipshod method. An accurate daily record was kept both as to the quantity and quality of the work done in order to guard against any personal prejudice on the part of the foreman and to insure absolute impartiality and justice for each inspector. In a comparatively short time this record enabled the foreman to stir the ambition of all the inspectors by increasing the wages of those who turned out a large quantity and good quality, while at the same time lowering the pay of those who did indifferent work and discharging others who proved to be incorrigibly slow or careless. A careful examination was then made of the way in which each girl spent her time and an accurate time study was undertaken, through the use of a stop-watch and record blanks, to determine how fast each kind of inspection should be done, and to establish the exact conditions under which each girl could do her quickest and best work, while at the same time guarding against giving her a task so severe that there was danger from over fatigue or exhaustion. This investigation showed that the girls spent a considerable part of their time either in partial idleness, talking and half working, or in actually doing nothing. Even when the hours of labor had been shortened from 1012 to 812 hours, a close observation of the girls showed that after about an hour and one-half of consecutive work they began to get nervous. They evidently needed a rest. It is wise to stop short of the point at which overstrain begins, so we arranged for them to have a ten minutes period for recreation at the end of each hour and one quarter. During these recess periods (two of ten minutes each in the morning and two in the afternoon) they were obliged to stop work and were encouraged to leave their seats and get a complete change of occupation by walking around and talking, etc.

In one respect no doubt some people will say that these girls were brutally treated. They were seated so far apart that they could not conveniently talk while at work.

Shortening their hours of labor, however, and providing so far as we knew the most favorable working conditions made it possible for them to really work steadily instead of pretending to do so. And it is only after this stage in the reorganization is reached, when the girls have been properly selected and on the one hand such precautions have been taken as to guard against the possibility of over-driving them, while, on the other hand, the temptation to slight their work has been removed and the most favorable working conditions have been established, that the final step should be taken which insures them what they most want, namely, *high wages*, and the employers what they most want, namely, the maximum output and best quality of work, – which means *a low labor cost.*

This step is to give each girl each day a carefully measured task which demands a full day's work from a competent operative, and also to give her a large premium or bonus whenever she accomplishes this task.

This was done in this case through establishing what is known as differential rate piece work. Under this system the pay of each girl was increased in proportion to the quantity of her output and also still more in proportion to the accuracy of her work.

As will be shown later, the differential rate (the lots inspected by the over-inspectors forming the basis for the differential) resulted in a large gain in the quantity of work done and at the same time in a marked improvement in the quality. Before they finally worked to the best advantage it was found to be necessary to measure the output of each girl as often as once every hour, and to send a teacher to each individual who was found to be falling behind to find what was wrong, to straighten her out, and to encourage and help her to catch up.

There is a general principle back of this which should be appreciated by all of those who are especially interested in the management of men.

A reward, if it is to be effective in stimulating men to do their best work, must come soon after the work has been done. But few men are able to look forward for more than a week or perhaps at most a month, and work hard for a reward which they are to receive at the end of this time.

The average workman must able to measure what he has accomplished and clearly see his reward at the end of each day if he is to do his best. And more elementary characters, such as the young girls inspecting bicycle balls, or *children*, for instance, should have proper encouragement either in the shape of personal attention from those over them or an actual reward in sight as often as once an hour.

This is one of the principal reasons why cooperation or "profit-sharing" either through selling stock to the employés or through dividends on wages received at the end of the year, etc., have been at the best only mildly effective in stimulating men to work hard. The nice time which they are sure to have to-day if they take things easily and go slowly proves more attractive than steady hard work with a possible reward to be shared with others six months later. A second reason for the inefficiency of profit-sharing schemes had been that no form of cooperation has yet been devised in which each individual is allowed free scope for his personal ambition. Personal ambition always has been and will remain a more powerful incentive to exertion than a desire for the general welfare. The few misplaced drones, who do the loafing and share equally in the profits, with the rest, under cooperation are sure to drag the better men down toward their level.

Other and formidable difficulties in the path of cooperative schemes are, the equitable division of the profits, and the fact that, while workmen are always ready to share the profits, they are neither able nor willing to share the losses. Further than this, in many cases, it is neither right nor just that they should share either the profits or the losses, since these may be due in great part to causes entirely beyond their influence or control, and to which they do not contribute.

To come back to the girls inspecting bicycle balls, however, the final outcome of all the changes was that *thirty-five girls did the work formerly done by one hundred and twenty*. And that the *accuracy of the work at the higher speed was two-thirds greater than at the former slow speed*. The good that came to the girls was:

First. That they averaged from 80 to 100 per cent. higher wages than they formerly received.

Second. Their hours-of-labor were shortened from 1012 to 812 per day, with a Saturday half holiday. And they were given four recreation periods properly distributed through the day, which made overworking impossible for a healthy girl.

Third. Each girl was made to feel that she was the object of especial care and interest on the part of the management, and that if anything went wrong with her she could always have a helper and teacher in the management to lean upon.

Fourth. All young women should be given two consecutive days of rest (with pay) each month, to be taken whenever they may choose. It is my impression that these girls were given this privilege, although I am not quite certain on this point.

The benefits which came to the company from these changes were:

First. A substantial improvement in the quality of the product.

Second. A material reduction in the cost of inspection, in spite of the extra expense involved in clerk work, teachers, time study, over-inspectors, and in paying higher wages.

Third. That the most friendly relations existed between the management and the employés, which rendered labor troubles of any kind or a strike impossible.

These good results were brought about by many changes which substituted favorable for unfavorable working conditions. It should be appreciated, however, that the one element which did more than all of the others was, the careful selection of girls with quick perception to replace those whose perceptions were slow – (the substitution of girls with a low personal coefficient for those whose personal coefficient was high) – the scientific selection of the workers.

The illustrations have thus far been purposely confined to the more elementary types of work, so that a very strong doubt must still remain as to whether this kind of cooperation is desirable in the case of more intelligent mechanics, that is, in the case of men who are more capable of generalization, and who would therefore be more likely, of their own volition, to choose the more scientific and better methods. The following illustrations will be given for the purpose of demonstrating the fact that in the higher classes of work the scientific laws which are developed are so intricate that the high-priced mechanic needs (even more than the cheap laborer) the cooperation of men better educated than himself in finding the laws, and then in selecting, developing, and training him to work in accordance with these laws. These illustrations should make perfectly clear our original proposition that in practically all of the mechanic arts the science which underlies each workman^s act is so great and amounts to so much that the workman who is best suited to actually doing the work is incapable, either through lack of education or through insufficient mental capacity, of understanding this science.

A doubt, for instance, will remain in the minds perhaps of most readers (in the case of an establishment which manufactures the same machine, year in and year out, in large quantities, and in which, therefore, each mechanic repeats the same limited series of operations over and over again), whether the ingenuity of each workman and the help which he from time to time receives from his foreman will not develop such superior methods and such a personal dexterity that no scientific study which could be made would result in a material increase in efficiency.

A number of years ago a company employing about three hundred men, which had been manufacturing the same machine for ten to fifteen years, sent for us to report as to whether any gain could be made through the introduction of scientific management. Their shops had been run for many years under a good superintendent and with excellent foremen and workmen, on piece work. The whole establishment was, without doubt, in better physical condition than the average machine-shop in this country. The superintendent was distinctly displeased when told that through the adoption of task management the output, with the same number of men and machines, could be more than doubled. He said that he believed that any such statement was mere boasting, absolutely false, and instead of inspiring him with confidence, he was disgusted that any one should make such an impudent claim. He, however, readily assented to the proposition that he should select any one of the machines whose output he considered as representing the average of the shop, and that we should then demonstrate on this machine that through scientific methods its output could be more than doubled.

The machine selected by him fairly represented the work of the shop. It had been run for ten or twelve years past by a first-class mechanic who was more than equal in his ability to the average workmen in the establishment. In a shop of this sort, in which similar machines are made over and over again, the work is necessarily greatly subdivided, so that no one man works upon more than a comparatively small number of parts during the year. A careful record was therefore made, in the presence of both parties, of the time actually taken in finishing each of the parts which this man worked upon. The total time required by him to finish each piece, as well as the exact speeds and feeds which he took, were noted, and a record was kept of the time which he took in setting the work in the machine and removing it. After obtaining in this way a statement of what represented a fair average of the work done in the shop, we applied to this one machine the principles of scientific management. By means of four quite elaborate slide-rules, which have been especially made for the purpose of determining the all-round capacity of metal-cutting machines, a careful analysis was made of every element of this machine in its relation to the work in hand. Its pulling power at its various speeds, its feeding capacity, and its proper speeds were determined by means of the slide-rules, and changes were then made in the countershaft and driving pulleys so as to run it at its proper speed. Tools, made of high- speed steel, and of the proper shapes, were properly dressed, treated, and ground. (It should be understood, however, that in this case the high-speed steel which had heretofore been in general use in the shop was also used in our demonstration.) A large special slide-rule was then made, by means of which the exact speeds and feeds were indicated at which each kind of work could be done in the shortest possible time in this particular lathe. After preparing in this way so that the workman should work according to the new method, one after another, pieces of work were finished in the lathe, corresponding to the work which had been done in our preliminary trials, and the gain in time made througt running the machine according to scientific principles ranged from two and one-half times the speed in the slowest instance to nine times the speed in the highest.

The change from rule-of-thumb management to scientific management involves, however, not only a study of what is the proper speed for doing the work and a remodeling of the tools and the implements in the shop, but also a complete change in the mental attitude of all the men in the shop toward their work and toward their employers. The physical improvements in the machines necessary to insure large gains, and the motion study followed by minute study with a stop-watch of the time in which each workman should do his work, can be made comparatively quickly. But the change in the mental attitude and in the habits of the three hundred or more workmen can be brought about only slowly and through a long series of object-lessons, which finally demonstrates to each man. The great advantage which he will gain by heartily cooperating in his every-day work with the men in the management. Within three years, however, in this shop, the output had been more than doubled per man and per machine. The men had been carefully selected and in almost all cases promoted from a lower to a higher order of work, and so instructed by their teachers (the functional foremen) that they were able to earn higher wages than ever before. The average increase in the daily earnings of each man was about 35 per cent., while, at the same time, the sum total of the wages paid for doing a given amount of work was lower than before. This increase in the speed of doing the work, of course, involved a substitution of the quickest hand methods for the old independent rule-of-thumb methods, and an elaborate analysis of the hand work done by each man. (By hand work is meant such work as depends upon the manual dexterity and speed of a workman, and which is independent of the work done by the machine.) The time saved by scientific hand work was in many cases greater even than that saved in machine-work.

It seems important to fully explain the reason why, with the aid of a slide-rule, and after having studied the art of cutting metals, it was possible for the scientifically equipped man, who had never before seen these particular jobs, and who had never worked on this machine, to do work from two and one-half to nine times as fast as it had been done before by a good mechanic who had spent his whole time for some ten to twelve years in doing this very work upon this particular machine. In a word, this was possible because the art of cutting metals involves a true science of no small magnitude, a science, in fact, so intricate that it is impossible for any machinist who is suited to running a lathe year in and year out either to understand it or to work according to its laws without the help of men who have made this their specialty. Men who are unfamiliar with machine-shop work are prone to look upon the manufacture of each piece as a special problem, independent of any other kind of machine-work. They are apt to think, for instance, that the problems connected with making the parts of an engine require the especial study, one may say almost the life study, of a set of engine-making mechanics, and that these problems are entirely different from those which would be met with in machining lathe or planer parts. In fact, however, a study of those elements which are peculiar either to engine parts or to lathe parts is trifling, compared with the great study of the art, or science, of cutting metals, upon a knowledge of which rests the ability to do really fast machine-work of all kinds. The real problem is how to remove chips fast from a casting or a forging, and how to make the piece smooth and true in the shortest time, and it matters but little whether the piece being worked upon is part, say, of a marine engine, a printing-press, or an automobile. For this reason, the man with the slide-rule, familiar with the science of cutting metals, who had never before seen this particular work, was able completely to distance the skilled mechanic who had made the parts of this machine his specialty for years.

It is true that whenever intelligent and educated men find that the responsibility for making progress in any of the mechanic arts rests with them, instead of upon the workmen who are actually laboring at the trade, that they almost invariably start on the road which leads to the development of a science where, in the past, has existed mere traditional or rule-of-thumb knowledge. When men, whose education has given them the habit of generalizing and everywhere looking for laws, find themselves confronted with a multitude of problems, such as exist in every trade and which have a general similarity one to another, it is inevitable that they should try to gather these problems into certain logical groups, and then search for some general laws or rules to guide them in their solution. As has been pointed out, however, the underlying principles of the management of "initiative and incentive," that is, the underlying philosophy of this management, necessarily leaves the solution of all of these problems in the hands of each individual workman, while the philosophy of scientific management places their solution in the hands of the management. The workman's whole time is each day taken in actually doing the work with his hands, so that, even if he had the necessary education and habits of generalizing in his thought, he lacks the time and the opportunity for developing these laws, because the study of even a simple law involving say time study requires the cooperation of two men, the one doing the work while the other times him with a stop-watch. And even if the workman were to develop laws where before existed only rule-of-thumb knowledge, his personal interest would lead him almost inevitably to keep his discoveries secret, so that he could, by means of this special knowledge, personally do more work than other men and so obtain higher wages. Under scientific management, on the other hand, it becomes the duty and also the pleasure of those who are engaged in the management not only to develop laws to replace rule of thumb, but also to teach impartially all of the workmen who are under them the quickest ways of working. The useful results obtained from these laws are always so great that any company can well afford to pay for the time and the experiments needed to develop them. Thus under scientific management exact scientific knowledge and methods are everywhere, sooner or later, sure to replace rule of thumb, whereas under the old type of management working in accordance with scientific laws is an impossibility. The development of the art or science of cutting metals is an apt illustration of this fact. In the fall of 1880, about the time that the writer started to make the experiments above referred to, to determine what constitutes a proper day's work for a laborer, he also obtained the permission of Mr. William Sellers, the President of the Midvale Steel Company, to make a series of experiments to determine what angles and shapes of tools were the best for cutting steel, and also to try to determine the proper cutting speed for steel. At the time that these experiments were started it was his belief that they would not last longer than six months, and, in fact, if it had been known that a longer period than this would be required, the permission to spend a considerable sum of money in making them would not have been forthcoming. A 66-inch diameter vertical boring-mill was the first machine used in making these experiments, and large locomotive tires, made out of hard steel of uniform quality, were day after day cut up into chips in gradually learning how to make, shape, and use the cutting tools so that they would do faster work. At the end of six months sufficient practical information had been obtained to far more than repay the cost of materials and wages which had been expended in experimenting. And yet the comparatively small number of experiments which had been made served principally to make it clear that the actual knowledge attained was but a small fraction of that which still remained to be developed, and which was badly needed by us, in our daily attempt to direct and help the machinists in their tasks.

Experiments in this field were carried on, with occasional interruption, through a period of about 26 years, in the course of which ten different experimental machines were especially fitted up to do this work. Between 30,000 and 50,000 experiments were carefully recorded, and many other experiments were made, of which no record was kept. In studying these laws more than 800,000 pounds of steel and iron was cut up into chips with the experimental tools, and it is estimated that from $150,000 to $200,000 was spent in the investigation.

Work of this character is intensely interesting to any one who has any love for scientific research. For the purpose of this paper, however, it should be fully appreciated that the motive power which kept these experiments going through many years, and which supplied the money and the opportunity for their accomplishment, was not an abstract search after scientific knowledge, but was the very practical fact that we lacked the exact information which was needed every day, in order to help our machinists to do their work in the best way and in the quickest time. All of these experiments were made to enable us to answer correctly the two questions which face every machinist each time that he does a piece of work in a metal-cutting machine, such as a lathe, planer, drill press, or milling machine. These two questions are:

- In order to do the work in the quickest time.
- At what cutting speed shall I run my machine? and What feed shall I use?

They sound so simple that they would appear to call for merely the trained judgment of any good mechanic. In fact, however, after working 26 years, it has been found that the answer in every case involves the solution of an intricate mathematical problem, in which the effect of twelve independent variables must be determined. Each of the twelve following variables has an important effect upon the answer. The figures which are given with each of the variables represent the effect of this element upon the cutting speed. For example, after the first variable (A) we quote, "The proportion is as 1 in the case of semi-hardened steel or chilled iron to 100 in the case of a very soft, low-carbon steel." The meaning of this quotation is that soft steel can be cut 100 times as fast as the hard steel or chilled iron. The ratios which are given, then, after each of these elements, indicate the wide range of judgment which practically every machinist has been called upon to exercise in the past in determining the best speed at which to run the machine and the best feed to use.

(A) The quality of the metal which is to be cut; *i.e.*, its hardness or other qualities which affect the cutting speed. The proportion is as 1 in the case of semi-hardened steel or chilled iron to 100 in the case of very soft, low-carbon steel.

(B) The chemical composition of the steel from which the tool is made, and the heat treatment of the tool. The proportion is as 1 in tools made from tempered carbon steel to 7 in the best high-speed tools.

(C) The thickness of the shaving, or, the thickness of the spiral strip or band of metal which is to be removed by the tool. The proportion is as 1 with thickness of shaving 316 of an inch to 312 with thickness of shaving 164 of an inch.

(D) The shape or contour of the cutting edge of the tool. The proportion is as 1 in a thread tool to 6 in a broad-nosed cutting tool.

(E) Whether a copious stream of water or other cooling medium is used on the tool. The proportion is as 1 for tool running dry to 1.41 for tool cooled by a copious stream of water.

(F) The depth of the cut. The proportion is as 1 with 12-inch depth of cut to 1.36 with 18-inch depth of cut.

(G) The duration of the cut, *i.e.*, the time which a tool must last under pressure of the shaving without being reground. The proportion is as 1 when tool is to be ground every 112 hours to 1.20 when tool is to be ground every 20 minutes.

(H) The lip and clearance angles of the tool. The proportion is as 1 with lip angle of 68 degrees to 1.023 with lip angle of 61 degrees.

(J) The elasticity of the work and of the tool on account of producing chatter. The proportion is as 1 with tool chattering to 1.15 with tool running smoothly.

(K) The diameter of the casting or forging which is being cut.

(L) The pressure of the chip or shaving upon the cutting surface of the tool.

(M) The pulling power and the speed and feed changes of the machine.

It may seem preposterous to many people that it should have required a period of 26 years to investigate the effect of these twelve variables upon the cutting speed of metals. To those, however, who have had personal experience as experimenters, it will be appreciated that the great difficulty of the problem lies in the fact that it contains so many variable elements. And in fact the great length of time consumed in making each single experiment was caused by the difficulty of holding eleven variables constant and uniform throughout the experiment, while the effect of the twelfth variable was being investigated. Holding the eleven variables constant was far more difficult than the investigation of the twelfth element. As, one after another, the effect upon the cutting speed of each of these variables was investigated, in order that practical use could be made of this knowledge, it was necessary to find a mathematical formula which expressed in concise form the laws which had been obtained. As examples of the twelve formulæ which were developed, the three following are given:

$$P=45{,}000D^{\frac{14}{15}}F^{\frac{3}{4}}$$

$$V=\frac{90}{T^{\frac{1}{8}}}$$

$$V=\frac{11.0}{F^{0.665}\left(\frac{48}{3}D\right)^{0.2373+\frac{2.4}{18+24D}}}$$

After these laws had been investigated and the various formulæ which mathematically expressed them had been determined, there still remained the difficult task of how to solve one of these complicated mathematical problems quickly enough to make this knowledge available for every-day use. If a good mathematician who had these formulæ before him were to attempt to get the proper answer (*i.e.*, to get the correct cutting speed and feed by working in the ordinary way) it would take him from two to six hours, say, to solve a single problem; far longer to solve the mathematical problem than would be taken in most cases by the workmen in doing the whole job in his machine. Thus a task of considerable magnitude which faced us was that of finding a quick solution of this problem, and as we made progress in its solution, the whole problem was from time to time presented by the writer to one after another of the noted mathematicians in this country. They were offered any reasonable fee for a rapid, practical method to be used in its solution. Some of these men merely glanced at it; others, for the sake of being courteous, kept it before them for some two or three weeks. They all gave us practically the same answer: that in many cases it was possible to solve mathematical problems which contained four variables, and in some cases problems with five or six variables, but that it was manifestly impossible to solve a problem containing twelve variables in any other way than by the slow process of "trial and error." A quick solution was, however, so much of a necessity in our every-day work of running machine-shops, that in spite of the small encouragement received from the mathematicians, we continued at irregular periods, through a term of fifteen years, to give a large amount of time searching for a simple solution. Four or five men at various periods gave practically their whole time to this work, and finally, while we were at the Bethlehem Steel Company, the slide-rule was developed which is illustrated on Folder No. 11 of the paper "On the Art of Cutting Metals," and is described in detail in the paper presented by Mr. Carl G. Barth to the American Society of Mechanical Engineers, entitled "Slide-rules for the Machine-shop, as a part of the Taylor System of Managements" (Vol. XXV of The Transactions of the American Society of Mechanical Engineers). By means of this slide-rule, one of these intricate problems can be solved in less than a half minute by any good mechanic, whether he understands anything about mathematics or not, thus making available for every-day, practical use the years of experimenting on the art of cutting metals. This is a good illustration of the fact that some way can always be found of making practical, everyday use of complicated scientific data, which appears to be beyond the experience and the range of the technical training of ordinary practical men. These slide-rules have been for years in constant daily use by machinists having no knowledge of mathematics.

A glance at the intricate mathematical formulæ (see page 109) which represent the laws of cutting metals should clearly show the reason why it is impossible for any machinist, without the aid of these laws, and who depends upon his personal experience, correctly to guess at the answer to the two questions:

- What speed shall I use?
- What feed shall I use?

Even though he may repeat the same piece of work many times. To return to the case of the machinist who had been working for ten to twelve years in machining the same pieces over and over again, there was but a remote chance in any of the various kinds of work which this man did that he should hit upon the one best method of doing each piece of work out of the hundreds of possible methods which lay before him. In considering this typical case, it must also be remembered that the metal-cutting machines throughout our machine-shops have practically all been speeded by their makers by guesswork, and without the knowledge obtained through a study of the art of cutting metals. In the machine-shops systematized by us we have found that there is not one machine in a hundred which is speeded by its makers at anywhere near the correct cutting speed. So that, in order to compete with the science of cutting metals, the machinist, before he could use proper speeds, would first have to put new pulleys on the countershaft of his machine, and also make in most cases changes in the shapes and treatment of his tools, etc. Many of these changes are matters entirely beyond his control, even if he knows what ought to be done. If the reason is clear to the reader why the rule-of-thumb knowledge obtained by the machinist who is engaged on *repeat work* cannot possibly compete with the true science of cutting metals, it should be even more apparent why the high-class mechanic, who is called upon to do a *great variety* of work from day to day, is even less able to compete with this science.

The high-class mechanic who does a different kind of work each day, in order to do each job in the quickest time, would need, in addition to a thorough knowledge of the art of cutting metals, a vast knowledge and experience in the quickest way of doing each kind of hand work. And the reader, by calling to mind the gain which was made by Mr. Gilbreth through his motion and time study in laying bricks, will appreciate the great possibilities for quicker methods of doing all kinds of hand work which lie before every tradesman after he has the help which comes from a scientific motion and time study of his work.

For nearly thirty years past, time-study men connected with the management of machine-shops have been devoting their whole time to a scientific motion study, followed by accurate time study, with a stop-watch, of all of the elements connected with the machinist's work. When, therefore, the teachers, who form one section of the management, and who are cooperating with the working men, are in possession both of the science of cutting metals and of the equally elaborate motion-study and time-study science connected with this work, it is not difficult to appreciate why even the highest class mechanic is unable to do his best work without constant daily assistance from his teachers. And if this fact has been made clear to the reader, one of the important objects in writing this paper will have been realized.

It is hoped that the illustrations which have been given make it apparent why scientific management must inevitably in all cases produce overwhelmingly greater results, both for the company and its employés, than can be obtained with the management of "initiative and incentive." And it should also be clear that these results have been attained, not through a marked superiority in the mechanism of one type of management over the mechanism of another, but rather through the substitution of one set of underlying principles for a totally different set of principles, – by the substitution of one philosophy for another philosophy in industrial management.

To repeat then throughout all of these illustrations, it will be seen that the useful results have hinged mainly upon (1) the substitution of a science for the individual judgment of the workman; (2) the scientific selection and development of the workman, after each man has been studied, taught, and trained, and one may say experimented with, instead of allowing the workmen to select themselves and develop in a haphazard way; and (3) the intimate cooperation of the management with the workmen, so that they together do the work in accordance with the scientific laws which have been developed, instead of leaving the solution of each problem in the hands of the individual workman. In applying these new principles, in place of the old individual effort of each workman, both sides share almost equally in the daily performance of each task, the management doing that part of the work for which they are best fitted, and the workmen the balance.

It is for the illustration of this philosophy that this paper has been written, but some of the elements involved in its general principles should be further discussed.

The development of a science sounds like a formidable undertaking, and in fact anything like a thorough study of a science such as that of cutting metals necessarily involves many years of work. The science of cutting metals, however, represents in its complication, and in the time required to develop it, almost an extreme case in the mechanic arts. Yet even in this very intricate science, within a few months after starting, enough knowledge had been obtained to much more than pay for the work of experimenting. This holds true in the case of practically all scientific development in the mechanic arts. The first laws developed for cutting metals were crude, and contained only a partial knowledge of the truth, yet this imperfect knowledge was vastly better than the utter lack of exact information or the very imperfect rule of thumb which existed before, and it enabled the workmen, with the help of the management, to do far quicker and better work. For example, a very short time was needed to discover one or two types of tools which, though imperfect as compared with the shapes developed years afterward, were superior to all other shapes and kinds in common use. These tools were adopted as standard and made possible an immediate increase in the speed of every machinist who used them. These types were superseded in a comparatively short time by still other tools which remained standard until they in their turn made way for later improvements.

The science which exists in most of the mechanic arts is, however, far simpler than the science of cutting metals. In almost all cases, in fact, the laws or rules which are developed are so simple that the average man would hardly dignify them with the name of a science. In most trades, the science is developed through a comparatively simple analysis and time study of the movements required by the workmen to do some small part of his work, and this study is usually made by a man equipped merely with a stop-watch and a properly ruled notebook. Hundreds of these "time-study men" are now engaged in developing elementary scientific knowledge where before existed only rule of thumb. Even the motion study of Mr. Gilbreth in bricklaying (described on pages 77 to 84) involves a much more elaborate investigation than that which occurs in most cases. The general steps to be taken in developing a simple law of this class are as follows:

First. Find, say, 10 or 15 different men (preferably in as many separate establishments and different parts of the country) who are especially skilful in doing the particular work to be analyzed.

Second. Study the exact series of elementary operations or motions which each of these men uses in doing the work which is being investigated, as well as the implements each man uses.

Third. Study with a stop-watch the time required to make each of these elementary movements and then select the quickest way of doing each element of the work.

Fourth. Eliminate all false movements, slow movements, and useless movements.

Fifth. After doing away with all unnecessary movements, collect into one series the quickest and best movements as well as the best implements.

This one new method, involving that series of motions which can be made quickest and best, is then substituted in place of the ten or fifteen inferior series which were formerly in use. This best method becomes standard, and remains standard, to be taught first to the teachers (or functional foremen) and by them to every workman in the establishment until it is superseded by a quicker and better series of movements. In this simple way one element after another of the science is developed.

In the same way each type of implement used in a trade is studied. Under the philosophy of the management of "initiative and incentive" each workman is called upon to use his own best judgment, so as to do the work in the quickest time, and from this results in all cases a large variety in the shapes and types of implements which are used for any specific purpose. Scientific management requires, first, a careful investigation of each of the many modifications of the same implement, developed under rule of thumb; and second, after a time study has been made of the speed attainable with each of these implements, that the good points of several of them shall be united in a single standard implement, which will enable the workman to work faster and with greater ease than he could before. This one implement, then, is adopted as standard in place of the many different kinds before in use, and it remains standard for all workmen to use until superseded by an implement which has been shown, through motion and time study, to be still better.

With this explanation it will be seen that the development of a science to replace rule of thumb is in most cases by no means a formidable undertaking, and that it can be accomplished by ordinary, every-day men without any elaborate scientific training; but that, on the other hand, the successful use of even the simplest improvement of this kind calls for records, system, and cooperation where in the past existed only individual effort.

There is another type of scientific investigation which has been referred to several times in this paper, and which should receive special attention, namely, the accurate study of the motives which influence men. At first it may appear that this is a matter for individual observation and judgment, and is not a proper subject for exact scientific experiments. It is true that the laws which result from experiments of this class, owing to the fact that the very complex organism – the human being – is being experimented with, are subject to a larger number of exceptions than is the case with laws relating to material things. And yet laws of this kind, which apply to a large majority of men, unquestionably exist, and when clearly defined are of great value as a guide in dealing with men. In developing these laws, accurate, carefully planned and executed experiments, extending through a term of years, have been made, similar in a general way to the experiments upon various other elements which have been referred to in this paper.

Perhaps the most important law belonging to this class, in its relation to scientific management, is the effect which the task idea has upon the efficiency of the workman. This, in fact, has become such an important element of the mechanism of scientific management, that by a great number of people scientific management has come to be known as "task management."

There is absolutely nothing new in the task idea. Each one of us will remember that in his own case this idea was applied with good results in his schoolboy days. No efficient teacher would think of giving a class of students an indefinite lesson to learn. Each day a definite, clear-cut task is set by the teacher before each scholar, stating that he must learn just so much of the subject; and it is only by this means that proper, systematic progress can be made by the students. The average boy would go very slowly if, instead of being given a task, he were told to do as much as he could. All of us are grown-up children, and it is equally true that the average workman will work with the greatest satisfaction, both to himself and to his employer, when he is given each day a definite task which he is to perform in a given time, and which constitutes a proper day's work for a good workman. This furnishes the workman with a clear-cut standard, by which he can throughout the day measure his own progress, and the accomplishment of which affords him the greatest satisfaction. The writer has described in other papers a series of experiments made upon workmen, which have resulted in demonstrating the fact that it is impossible, through any long period of time, to get workmen to work much harder than the average men around them, unless they are assured a large and a permanent increase in their pay. This series of experiments, however, also proved that plenty of workmen can be found who are willing to work at their best speed, provided they are given this liberal increase in wages. The workman must, however, be fully assured that this increase beyond the average is to be permanent. Our experiments have shown that the exact percentage of increase required to make a workman work at his highest speed depends upon the kind of work which the man is doing.

It is absolutely necessary, then, when workmen are daily given a task which calls for a high rate of speed on their part, that they should also be insured the necessary high rate of pay whenever they are successful. This involves not only fixing for each man his daily task, but also paying him a large bonus, or premium, each time that he succeeds in doing his task in the given time. It is difficult to appreciate in full measure the help which the proper use of these two elements is to the workman in elevating him to the highest standard of efficiency and speed in his trade, and then keeping him there, unless one has seen first the old plan and afterward the new tried upon the same man. And in fact until one has seen similar accurate experiments made upon various grades of workmen engaged in doing widely different types of work. The remarkable and almost uniformly good results from the *correct* application of the task and the bonus must be seen to be appreciated. These two elements, the task and the bonus (which, as has been pointed out in previous papers, can be applied in several ways), constitute two of the most important elements of the mechanism of scientific management. They are especially important from the fact that they are, as it were, a climax, demanding before they can be used almost all of the other elements of the mechanism; such as a planning department, accurate time study, standardization of methods and implements, a routing system, the training of functional foremen or teachers, and in many cases instruction cards, slide-rules, etc. The necessity for systematically teaching workmen how to work to the best advantage has been several times referred to. It seems desirable, therefore, to explain in rather more detail how this teaching is done. In the case of a machine-shop which is managed under the modern system, detailed written instructions as to the best way of doing each piece of work are prepared in advance, by men in the planning department. These instructions represent the combined work of several men in the planning room, each of whom has his own specialty, or function. One of them, for instance, is a specialist on the proper speeds and cutting tools to be used. He uses the slide-rules which have been above described as an aid, to guide him in obtaining proper speeds, etc. Another man analyzes the best and quickest motions to be made by the workman in setting the work up in the machine and removing it, etc. Still a third, through the time-study records which have been accumulated, makes out a timetable giving the proper speed for doing each element of the work. The directions of all of these men, however, are written on a single instruction card, or sheet.

These men of necessity spend most of their time in the planning department, because they must be close to the records and data which they continually use in their work, and because this work requires the use of a desk and freedom from interruption. Human nature is such, however, that many of the workmen, if left to themselves, would pay but little attention to their written instructions. It is necessary, therefore, to provide teachers (called functional foremen) to see that the workmen both understand and carry out these written instructions.

Under functional management, the old-fashioned single foreman is superseded by eight different men, each one of whom has his own special duties, and these men, acting as the agents for the planning department (see paragraph 234 to 245 of the paper entitled "Shop Management"), are the expert teachers, who are at all times in the shop, helping and directing the workmen. Being each one chosen for his knowledge and personal skill in his specialty, they are able not only to tell the workman what he should do, but in case of necessity they do the work themselves in the presence of the workman, so as to show him not only the best but also the quickest methods. One of these teachers (called the inspector) sees to it that he understands the drawings and instructions for doing the work. He teaches him how to do work of the right quality; how to make it fine and exact where it should be fine, and rough and quick where accuracy is not required, – the one being just as important for success as the other. The second teacher (the gang boss) shows him how to set up the job in his machine, and teaches him to make all of his personal motions in the quickest and best way. The third (the speed boss) sees that the machine is run at the best speed and that the proper tool is used in the particular way which will enable the machine to finish its product in the shortest possible time. In addition to the assistance given by these teachers, the workman receives orders and help from four other men; from the "repair boss" as to the adjustment, cleanliness, and general care of his machine, belting, etc.; from the "time clerk," as to everything relating to his pay and to proper written reports and returns; from the "route clerk," as to the order in which he does his work and as to the movement of the work from one part of the shop to another; and, in case a workman gets into any trouble with any of his various bosses, the "disciplinarian" interviews him.

It must be understood, of course, that all workmen engaged on the same kind of work do not require the same amount of individual teaching and attention from the functional foremen. The men who are new at a given operation naturally require far more teaching and watching than those who have been a long time at the same kind of jobs.

Now, when through all of this teaching and this minute instruction the work is apparently made so smooth and easy for the workman, the first impression is that this all tends to make him a mere automaton, a wooden man. As the workmen frequently say when they first come under this system, "Why, I am not allowed to think or move without some one interfering or doing it for me!" The same criticism and objection, however, can be raised against all other modern subdivision of labor. It does not follow, for example, that the modern surgeon is any more narrow or wooden a man than the early settler of this country. The frontiersman, however, had to be not only a surgeon, but also an architect, housebuilder, lumberman, farmer, soldier, and doctor, and he had to settle his law cases with a gun. You would hardly say that the life of the modern surgeon is any more narrowing, or that he is more of a wooden man than the frontiersman. The many problems to be met and solved by the surgeon are just as intricate and difficult and as developing and broadening in their way as were those of the frontiersman.

And it should be remembered that the training of the surgeon has been almost identical in type with the teaching and training which is given to the workman under scientific management. The surgeon, all through his early years, is under the closest supervision of more experienced men, who show him in the minutest way how each element of his work is best done. They provide him with the finest implements, each one of which has been the subject of special study and development, and then insist upon his using each of these implements in the very best way. All of this teaching, however, in no way narrows him. On the contrary he is quickly given the very best knowledge of his predecessors; and, provided (as he is, right from the start) with standard implements and methods which represent the best knowledge of the world up to date, he is able to use his own originality and ingenuity to make *real additions to the world's knowledge, instead of reinventing things which are old.* In a similar way the workman who is cooperating with his many teachers under scientific management has an opportunity to develop which is at least as good as and generally better than that which he had when the whole problem was "up to him" and he did his work entirely unaided.

If it were true that the workman would develop into a larger and finer man without all of this teaching, and without the help of the laws which have been formulated for doing his particular job, then it would follow that the young man who now comes to college to have the help of a teacher in mathematics, physics, chemistry, Latin, Greek, etc., would do better to study these things unaided and by himself. The only difference in the two cases is that students come to their teachers, while from the nature of the work done by the mechanic under scientific management, the teachers must go to him. What really happens is that, with the aid of the science which is invariably developed, and through the instructions from his teachers, each workman of a given intellectual capacity is enabled to do a much higher, more interesting, and finally more developing and more profitable kind of work than he was before able to do. The laborer who before was unable to do anything beyond, perhaps, shoveling and wheeling dirt from place to place, or carrying the work from one part of the shop to another, is in many cases taught to do the more elementary machinist's work, accompanied by the agreeable surroundings and the interesting variety and higher wages which go with the machinist's trade. The cheap machinist or helper, who before was able to run perhaps merely a drill press, is taught to do the more intricate and higher priced lathe and planer work, while the highly skilled and more intelligent machinists become functional foremen and teachers. And so on, right up the line.

It may seem that with scientific management there is not the same incentive for the workman to use his ingenuity in devising new and better methods of doing the work as well as in improving his implements, that there is with the old type of management. It is true that with scientific management the workman is not allowed to use whatever implements and methods he sees fit in the daily practise of his work. Every encouragement, however, should be given him to suggest improvements, both in methods and in implements. And whenever a workman proposes an improvement, it should be the policy of the management to make a careful analysis of the new method, and if necessary conduct a series of experiments to determine accurately the relative merit of the new suggestion and of the old standard. And whenever the new method is found to be markedly superior to the old, it should be adopted as the standard for the whole establishment. The workman should be given the full credit for the improvement, and should be paid a cash premium as a reward for his ingenuity. In this way the true initiative of the workmen is better attained under scientific management than under the old individual plan.

The history of the development of scientific management up to date, calls for a word of warning. The mechanism of management must not be mistaken for its essence, or underlying philosophy. Precisely the same mechanism will in one case produce disastrous results and in another the most beneficent. The same mechanism which will produce the finest results when made to serve the underlying principles of scientific management, will lead to failure and disaster if accompanied by the wrong spirit in those who are using it. Hundreds of people have already mistaken the mechanism of this system for its essence. Messrs. Gantt, Barth, and the writer have presented papers to the American Society of Mechanical Engineers on the subject of scientific management. In these papers the mechanism which is used has been described at some length. As elements of this mechanism may be cited:

- Time study, with the implements and methods for properly making it.
- Functional or divided foremanship and its superiority to the old-fashioned single foreman.
- The standardization of all tools and implements used in the trades, and also of the acts or movements of workmen for each class of work.
- The desirability of a planning room or department.
- The "exception principle" in management.
- The use of slide-rules and similar time-saving implements.
- Instruction cards for the workman.
- The task idea in management, accompanied by a large bonus for the successful performance of the task.
- The "differential rate."
- Mnemonic systems for classifying manufactured products as well as implements used in manufacturing.
- A routing system.
- Modern cost system, etc., etc.

These are, however, merely the elements or details of the mechanism of management. Scientific management, in its essence, consists of a certain philosophy, which results, as before stated, in a combination of the four great underlying principles of management: When, however, the elements of this mechanism, such as time study, functional foremanship, etc., are used without being accompanied by the true philosophy of management, the results are in many cases disastrous. And, unfortunately, even when men who are thoroughly in sympathy with the principles of scientific management undertake to change too rapidly from the old type to the new, without heeding the warnings of those who have had years of experience in making this change, they frequently meet with serious troubles, and sometimes with strikes, followed by failure.

The writer, in his paper on "Shop Management," has called especial attention to the risks which managers run in attempting to change rapidly from the old to the new management. In many cases, however, this warning has not been heeded. The physical changes which are needed, the actual time study which has to be made, the standardization of all implements connected with the work, the necessity for individually studying each machine and placing it in perfect order, all take time, but the faster these elements of the work are studied and improved, the better for the undertaking. On the other hand, the really great problem involved in a change from the management of "initiative and incentive" to scientific management consists in a complete evolution in the mental attitude and the habits of all of those engaged in the management, as well of the workmen. And this change can be brought about only gradually and through the presentation of many object-lessons to the workman, which, together with the teaching which "he receives, thoroughly convince him of the superiority of the new over the old way of doing the work. This change in the mental attitude of the workman imperatively demands time. It is impossible to hurry it beyond a certain speed. The writer has over and over again warned those who contemplated making this change that it was a matter, even in a simple establishment, of from two to three years, and that in some cases it requires from four to five years.

The first few changes which affect the workmen should be made exceedingly slowly, and only one workman at a time should be dealt with at the start. Until this single man has been thoroughly convinced that a great gain has come to him from the new method, no further change should be made. Then one man after another should be tactfully changed over. After passing the point at which from one-fourth to one-third of the men in the employ of the company have been changed from the old to the new, very rapid progress can be made, because at about this time there is, generally, a complete revolution in the public opinion of the whole establishment and practically all of the workmen who are working under the old system become desirous to share in the benefits which they see have been received by those working under the new plan.

Inasmuch as the writer has personally retired from the business of introducing this system of management (that is, from all work done in return for any money compensation), he does not hesitate again to emphasize the fact that those companies are indeed fortunate who can secure the services of experts who have had the necessary practical experience in introducing scientific management, and who have made a special study of its principles. It is not enough that a man should have been a manager in an establishment which is run under the new principles. The man who undertakes to direct the steps to be taken in changing from the old to the new (particularly in any establishment doing elaborate work) must have had personal experience in overcoming the especial difficulties which are always met with, and which are peculiar to this period of transition. It is for this reason that the writer expects to devote the rest of his life chiefly to trying to help those who wish to take up this work as their profession, and to advising the managers and owners of companies in general as to the steps which they should take in making this change.

As a warning to those who contemplate adopting scientific management, the following instance is given. Several men who lacked the extended experience which is required to change without danger of strikes, or without interference with the success of the business, from the management of "initiative and incentive" to scientific management, attempted rapidly to increase the output in quite an elaborate establishment, employing between three thousand and four thousand men. Those who undertook to make this change were men of unusual ability, and were at the same time enthusiasts and I think had the interests of the workmen truly at heart. They were, however, warned by the writer, before starting, that they must go exceedingly slowly, and that the work of making the change in this establishment could not be done in less than from three to five years. This warning they entirely disregarded. They evidently believed that by using much of the mechanism of scientific management, in combination with the principles of the management of "initiative and incentive," instead of with the principles of scientific management, that they could do, in a year or two, what had been proved in the past to require at least double this time. The knowledge obtained from accurate time study, for example, is a powerful implement, and can be used, in one case to promote harmony between the workmen and the management, by gradually educating, training, and leading the workmen into new and better methods of doing the work, or, in the other case, it may be used more or less as a club to drive the workmen into doing a larger day^s work for approximately the same pay that they received in the past. Unfortunately the men who had charge of this work did not take the time and the trouble required to train functional foremen, or teachers, who were fitted gradually to lead and educate the workmen. They attempted, through the old-style foreman, armed with his new weapon (accurate time study), to drive the workmen, against their wishes, and without much increase in pay, to work much harder, instead of gradually teaching and leading them toward new methods, and convincing them through object-lessons that task management means for them somewhat harder work, but also far greater prosperity. The result of all this disregard of fundamental principles was a series of strikes, followed by the downfall of the men who attempted to make the change, and by a return to conditions throughout the establishment far worse than those which existed before the effort was made.

This instance is cited as an object-lesson of the futility of using the mechanism of the new management while leaving out its essence, and also of trying to shorten a necessarily long operation in entire disregard of past experience. It should be emphasized that the men who undertook this work were both able and earnest, and that failure was not due to lack of ability on their part, but to their undertaking to do the impossible. These particular men will not again make a similar mistake, and it is hoped that their experience may act as a warning to others.

In this connection, however, it is proper to again state that during the thirty years that we have been engaged in introducing scientific management there has not been a single strike from those who were working in accordance with its principles, even during the critical period when the change was being made from the old to the new. If proper methods are used by men who have had experience in this work, there is absolutely no danger from strikes or other troubles.

The writer would again insist that in no case should the managers of an establishment, the work of which is elaborate, undertake to change from the old to the new type unless the directors of the company fully understand and believe in the fundamental principles of scientific management and unless they appreciate all that is involved in making this change, particularly the time required, and unless they want scientific management greatly.

Doubtless some of those who are especially interested in working men will complain because under scientific management the workman, when he is shown how to do twice as much work as he formerly did, is not paid twice his former wages, while others who are more interested in the dividends than the workmen will complain that under this system the men receive much higher wages than they did before. It does seem grossly unjust when the bare statement is made that the competent pig-iron handler, for instance, who has been so trained that he piles 3610 times as much iron as the incompetent man formerly did, should receive an increase of only 60 per cent. in wages.

It is not fair, however, to form any final judgment until all of the elements in the case have been considered. At the first glance we see only two parties to the transaction, the workmen and their employers. We overlook the third great party, the whole people, – the consumers, who buy the product of the first two and who ultimately pay both the wages of the workmen and the profits of the employers. The rights of the people are therefore greater than those of either employer or employé. And this third great party should be given its proper share of any gain. In fact, a glance at industrial history shows that in the end the whole people receive the greater part of the benefit coming from industrial improvements. In the past hundred years, for example, the greatest factor tending toward increasing the output, and thereby the prosperity of the civilized world, has been the introduction of machinery to replace hand labor.

And without doubt the greatest gain through this change has come to the whole people – the consumer. Through short periods, especially in the case of patented apparatus, the dividends of those who have introduced new machinery have been greatly increased, and in many cases, though unfortunately not universally, the employés have obtained materially higher wages, shorter hours, and better working conditions. But in the end the major part of the gain has gone to the whole people.

And this result will follow the introduction of scientific management just as surely as it has the introduction of machinery.

To return to the case of the pig-iron handler. We must assume, then, that the larger part of the gain which has come from his great increase in output will in the end go to the people in the form of cheaper pig-iron. And before deciding upon how the balance is to be divided between the workmen and the employer, as to what is just and fair compensation for the man who does the piling and what should be left for the company as profit, we must look at the matter from all sides.

First. As we have before stated, the pig-iron handler is not an extraordinary man difficult to find, he is merely a man more or less of the type of the ox, heavy both mentally and physically.

Second. The work which this man does tires him no more than any healthy normal- laborer is tired by a proper day's work. (If this man is overtired by his work, then the task has been wrongly set and this is as far as possible from the object of scientific management.)

Third. It was not due to this man's initiative or originality that he did his big day's work, but to the knowledge of the science of pig-iron handling developed and taught him by some one else.

Fourth. It is just and fair that men of the same general grade (when their all-round capacities are considered) should be paid about the same wages when they are all working to the best of their abilities. (It would be grossly unjust to other laborers, for instance, to pay this man 3610 as high wages as other men of his general grade receive for an honest full day's work.)

Fifth. As is explained (page 74), the 60 per cent. increase in pay which he received was not the result of an arbitrary judgment of a foreman or superintendent, it was the result of a long series of careful experiments impartially made to determine what compensation is really for the man's true and best interest when all things are considered.

Thus we see that the pig-iron handler with his 60 per cent. increase in wages is not an object for pity but rather a subject for congratulation. After all, however, facts are in many cases more convincing than opinions or theories, and it is a significant fact that those workmen who have come under this system during the past thirty years have invariably been satisfied with the increase in pay which they have received, while their employers have been equally pleased with their increase in dividends. The writer is one of those who believes that more and more will the third party (the whole people), as it becomes acquainted with the true facts, insist that justice shall be done to all three parties. It will demand the largest efficiency from both employers and employés. It will no longer tolerate the type of employer who has his eye on dividends alone, who refuses to do his full share of the work and who merely cracks his whip over the heads of his workmen and attempts to drive them into harder work for low pay.

No more will it tolerate tyranny on the part of labor which demands one increase after another in pay and shorter hours while at the same time it becomes less instead of more efficient. And the means which the writer firmly believes will be adopted to bring about, first, efficiency both in employer and employé and then an equitable division of the profits of their joint efforts will be scientific management, which has for its sole aim the attainment of justice for all three parties through impartial scientific investigation of all the elements of the problem. For a time both sides will rebel against this advance. The workers will resent any interference with their old rule-of-thumb methods, and the management will resent being asked to take on new duties and burdens; but in the end the people through enlightened public opinion will force the new order of things upon both employer and employé.

It will doubtless be claimed that in all that has been said no new fact has been brought to light that was not known to some one in the past. Very likely this is true. Scientific management does not necessarily involve any great invention, nor the discovery of new or startling facts. It does, however, involve a certain *combination* of elements which have not existed in the past, namely, old knowledge so collected, analyzed, grouped, and classified into laws and rules that it constitutes a science; accompanied by a complete change in the mental attitude of the working men as well as of those on the side of the management, toward each other, and toward their respective duties and responsibilities. Also, a new division of the duties between the two sides and intimate, friendly cooperation to an extent that is impossible under the philosophy of the old management. And even all of this in many cases could not exist without the help of mechanisms which have been gradually developed. It is no single element, but rather this whole combination, that constitutes scientific management, which may be summarized as:

- Science, not rule of thumb.
- Harmony, not discord.
- Cooperation, not individualism.
- Maximum output, in place of restricted output.

- The development of each man to his greatest efficiency and prosperity.

The writer wishes to again state that: "The time is fast going by for the great personal or individual achievement of any one man standing alone and without the help of those around him. And the time is coming when all great things will be done by that type of cooperation in which each man performs the function for which he is best suited, each man preserves his own individuality and is supreme in his particular function, and each man at the same time loses none of his originality and proper personal initiative, and yet is controlled by and must work harmoniously with many other men." The examples given above of the increase in output realized under the new management fairly represent the gain which is possible. They do not represent extraordinary or exceptional cases, and have been selected from among thousands of similar illustrations which might have been given. Let us now examine the good which would follow the general adoption of these principles.

The larger profit would come to the whole world in general.

The greatest material gain which those of the present generation have over past generations has come from the fact that the average man in this generation, with a given expenditure of effort, is producing two times, three times, even four times as much of those things that are of use to man as it was possible for the average man in the past to produce. This increase in the productivity of human effort is, of course, due to many causes, besides the increase in the personal dexterity of the man. It is due to the discovery of steam and electricity, to the introduction of machinery, to inventions, great and small, and to the progress in science and education. But from whatever cause this increase in productivity has come, it is to the greater productivity of each individual that the *whole country* owes its greater prosperity.

Those who are afraid that a large increase in the productivity of each workman will throw other men out of work, should realize that the one element more than any other which differentiates civilized from uncivilized countries – prosperous from poverty-stricken peoples – is that the average man in the one is five or six times as productive as the other. It is also a fact that the chief cause for the large percentage of the unemployed in England (perhaps the most virile nation in the world), is that the workmen of England, more than in any other civilized country, are deliberately restricting their output because they are possessed by the fallacy that it is against their best interest for each man to work as hard as he can.

The general adoption of scientific management would readily in the future double the productivity of the average man engaged in industrial work. Think of what this means to the whole country. Think of the increase, both in the necessities and luxuries of life, which becomes available for the whole country, of the possibility of shortening the hours of labor when this is desirable, and of the increased opportunities for education, culture, and recreation which this implies. But while the whole world would profit by this increase in production, the manufacturer and the workman will be far more interested in the especial local gain that comes to them and to the people immediately around them. Scientific management will mean, for the employers and the workmen who adopt it – and particularly for those who adopt it first – the elimination of almost all causes for dispute and disagreement between them. What constitutes a fair day's work will be a question for scientific investigation, instead of a subject to be bargained and haggled over. Soldiering will cease because the object for soldiering will no longer exist. The great increase in wages which accompanies this type of management will largely eliminate the wage question as a source of dispute. But more than all other causes, the close, intimate cooperation, the constant personal contact between the two sides, will tend to diminish friction and discontent. It is difficult for two people whose interests are the same, and who work side by side in accomplishing the same object, all day long, to keep up a quarrel.

The low cost of production which accompanies a doubling of the output will enable the companies who adopt this management, particularly those who adopt it first, to compete far better than they were able to before, and this will so enlarge their markets that their men will have almost constant work even in dull times, and that they will earn larger profits at all times.

This means increase in prosperity and diminution in poverty, not only for their men but for the whole community immediately around them. As one of the elements incident to this great gain in output, each workman has been systematically trained to his highest state of efficiency, and has been taught to do a higher class of work than he was able to do under the old types of management; and at the same time he has acquired a friendly mental attitude toward his employers and his whole working conditions, whereas before a considerable part of his time was spent in criticism, suspicious watchfulness, and sometimes in open warfare. This direct gain to all of those working under the system is without doubt the most important single element in the whole problem. Is not the realization of results such as these of far more importance than the solution of most of the problems which are now agitating both the English and American peoples? And is it not the duty of those who are acquainted with these facts, to exert themselves to make the whole community realize this importance?

* * *

The author is constantly in receipt of letters asking for a list of the companies who are working under scientific management. It would be highly improper to furnish any one with a list of this kind. Many of those companies who have introduced scientific management would seriously object to answering the letters which would be showered upon them if such a list were given out. On the other hand, there are certain companies who are willing to take the trouble to answer such letters.

To all of those who are sufficiently interested in scientific management, the writer would most heartily extend an invitation to come to his house when they are in the neighborhood of Philadelphia. He will be glad to show them the details of scientific management as it is practised in several establishments in Philadelphia. Inasmuch as the greater part of the writer's time is given up to forwarding the cause of scientific management, he regards visits of this sort as a privilege, rather than as an intrusion.

- The writer has tried to make the reason for this unfortunate state of things clear in a paper entitled "Shop Management," read before the American Society of Mechanical Engineers."
- For example, the records containing the data used under scientific management in an ordinary machine-shop fill thousands of pages.
- Many people have questioned the accuracy of the statement that first-class workmen can load 4712 tons of pig iron from the ground on to a car in a day. For those who are skeptical, therefore, the following data relating to this work are given:

First. That our experiments indicated the existence of the following law: that a first-class laborer, suited to such work as handling pig iron, could be under load only 42 per cent. of the day and must be free from load 58 per cent, of the day.

Second. That a man in loading pig iron from piles placed on the ground in an open field on to a car which stood on a track adjoining these piles, ought to handle (and that they did handle regularly) 4712 long tons (2240 pounds per ton) per day.

That the price paid for loading this pig iron was 910 cents per ton, and that the men working at it averaged $1.85 per day, whereas, in the past, they had been paid only $1.15 per day. In addition to these facts, the following are given:

- 4712 long tons equal 106,400 pounds of pig iron per day. At 92 pounds per pig, equals 1156 pigs per day.

- 42 per cent, of a day under load equals 600 minutes; multiplied by 0.42 equals 252 minutes under load.

- 252 minutes divided by 1156 pigs equals 0.22 minutes per pig under load.

A pig-iron handler walks on the level at the rate of one foot in 0.006 minutes. The average distance of the piles of pig iron from the car was 36 feet. It is a fact, however, that many of the pig-iron handlers ran with their pig as soon as they reached the inclined plank. Many of them also would run down the plank after loading the car. So that when the actual loading went on, many of them moved at a faster rate than is indicated by the above figures. Practically the men were made to take a rest, generally by sitting down, after loading ten to twenty pigs. This rest was in addition to the time which it took them to walk back from the car to the pile. It is likely that many of those who are skeptical about the possibility of loading this amount of pig iron do not realize that while these men were walking back they were entirely free from load, and that therefore their muscles had, during that time, the opportunity for recuperation. It will be noted that with an average distance of 36 feet of the pig iron from the car, these men walked about eight miles under load each day and eight miles free from load. If any one who is interested in these figures will multiply them and divide them, one into the other, in various ways, he will find that all of the facts stated check up exactly.

See paper read before the *American Society of Mechanical Engineers*, by Fred. W. Taylor, Vol. XVI, p. 856, entitled "Piece Rate System."

Time and again the experimenter in the mechanic arts will find himself face to face with the problem as to whether he had better make immediate practical use of the knowledge which he has attained, or wait until some positive finality in his conclusions has been reached. He recognizes clearly the fact that he has already made some definite progress, but sees the possibility (even the probability) of still further improvement. Each particular case must of course be independently considered, but the general conclusion we have reached is that in most instances it is wise to put one's conclusions as soon as possible to the rigid test of practical use. The one indispensable condition for such a test, however, is that the experimenter shall have full opportunity, coupled with sufficient authority, to insure a thorough and impartial trial. And this, owing to the almost universal prejudice in favor of the old, and to the suspicion of the new, is difficult to get.

- *First.* The development of a true science.
- *Second.* The scientific selection of the workman.
- *Third.* His scientific education and development.
- *Fourth.* Intimate friendly cooperation between the management and the men.

260 Pages
Paperback
ISBN: 978-1-9991585-1-4

The complete Series of *The Wealth of Nations*
published by *1st. Page Classics*

Book I
Of the Causes of Improvement in the productive Powers of Labour, and of the Order according to which its Produce is naturally distributed among the different Ranks of the People
260 pages, Paperback
ISBN: 978-1-9991585-1-4

Book II + III
Of the Nature, Accumulation, and Employment of Stock of the different Progress of Opulence in different Nations
152 pages, Paperback
ISBN:: 978-1-9991585-2-1

Book IV
Of Systems of political Economy
280 pages, Paperback
ISBN: 978-1-9991585-3-8

Book V
Of the Revenue of the Sovereign or Commonwealth
284 pages, Paperback
ISBN: 978-1-9991585-4-5

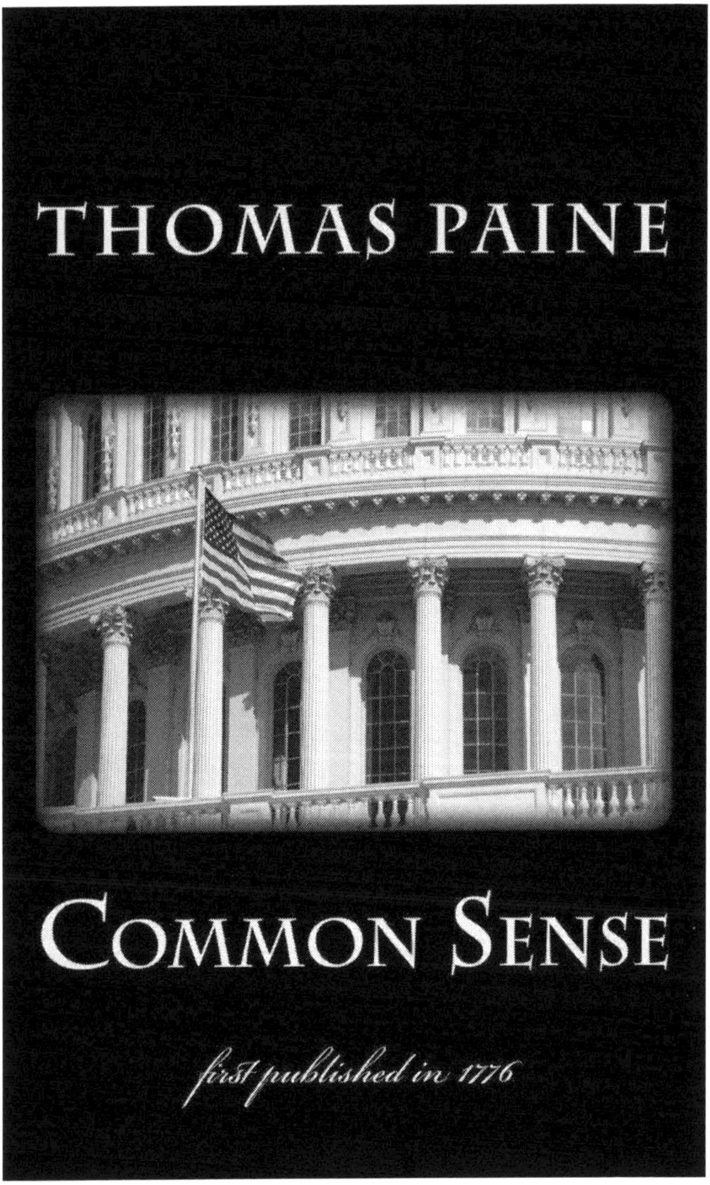

76 Pages
eBook & Paperback
ISBN: 978-1-9758-5555-0

Printed in Great Britain
by Amazon

54498627R00064

Printed in Great Britain
by Amazon

54498627R00064